D1051849

BUSINESS REPLY MAIL

FIRST CLASS MAIL   PERMIT NO 23   LAYTON, UT

POSTAGE WILL BE PAID BY THE ADDRESSEE

Veg Out
vegetarian
Guide®
P.O. BOX 667
LAYTON, UT 84041

Veg Out vegetarian Guide®

Your Name _____

Address _____

Phone Number _____

E-mail _____

Restaurant You Are Recommending

Name _____

Address _____

Phone Number _____

Recommended dishes _____

Comments _____

_____

_____

_____

If this restaurant is chosen for an upcoming edition of a VegOut! guide, you will receive a free copy of that guide.

Veg Out
Out
Vegetarian Guide®

Coming Fall 2004!

VegOut:
Vegetarian
Guide® to
Seattle and
Portland
$12.95 Paperback with
Foldout Map
1-58685-441-0

VegOut:
Vegetarian
Guide® to
Washington, D.C.
$12.95 Paperback with
Foldout Map
1-58685-471-2

Veg Out

Vegetarian Guide® to

San Francisco Bay Area

Michele Anna Jordan

Gibbs Smith, Publisher
Salt Lake City

First Edition
08 07 06 05 04   10 9 8 7 6 5 4 3 2 1

Published by
Gibbs Smith, Publisher
P.O. Box 667
Layton, Utah 84041

Orders: (1-800) 748-5439
www.gibbs-smith.com

Cover design by Kurt Wahlner
Interior design by Frederick Schneider/Grafis
Printed and bound in China

Library of Congress Cataloging-in-Publication Data

Jordan, Michele Anna.
Vegout! : vegetarian guide to San Francisco Bay
area / Michele Anna Jordan.—1st ed.
p. cm.
ISBN 1-58685-383-X
1. Vegetarian cookery. 2. Cookery—California—San Francisco
Bay Area.
I. Title.
TX837.J574 2004
641.5'636—dc22
                            2004002127

CONTENTS

FOREWORD 6

PREFACE 7

ACKNOWLEDGMENTS 9

ABOUT THIS BOOK 10

RESTAURANTS 11

    Alameda County 11

    Berkeley and Oakland 15

    Marin County 41

    Mendocino and Lake Counties 53

    Napa and Contra Costa Counties 57

    San Francisco 67

    San Mateo County 115

    Santa Clara and Santa Cruz Counties 125

    Sonoma County 145

CERTIFIED FARMERS MARKETS 165

GREEN GROCERS 171

JUICE BARS, CHEESE SHOPS, BAKERIES 178

COOKING SCHOOLS AND CLASSES 181

VEGETARIAN SOCIETIES 182

INDEXES 185

    Alphabetical Index 185

    Cuisine Index 187

    Top 10 191

FOREWORD

Gibbs Smith, Publisher, is thrilled to have the opportunity to initiate a series of vegetarian and vegan guides to major cities and regions throughout the United States and the world. Our primary goal is to have the guides be useful to consumers as they explore their own communities and travel near and far in search of the finest quality vegetarian and vegan fare.

We also hope to encourage and celebrate established vegetarian and vegan communities and to invite their exploration by many more people. Our objective is to further the pleasurable and health-giving effects of vegetarian and vegan dining.

We encourage you to use the guides and to be part of the creation of future guides in the series, as we revise and update each edition. As you discover new or established vegetarian or vegan restaurants that deserve the attention of others, please let us know. Either e-mail us at vegout@gibbs-smith.com or fill out and mail the reply card found in the back of the guides. If your recommended restaurant is chosen for an upcoming edition of *VegOut*, we'll send you a copy of that new edition free.

Happy eating!

PREFACE

The Bay Area is an easy place for vegetarians to enjoy a meal, as it is the rare restaurant that will not accommodate most of the myriad dietary requests they receive daily. The better the restaurant, the more gracious the accommodation will be. If you do not see something that suits you, be sure to ask your server. Sometimes the off-menu vegetarian offerings are even better than what is on the menu. A word of caution: Please be brief and to the point, treat your server as you wish to be treated, and don't flaunt your philosophy or your food issues, as servers are always busy, whether they appear so or not.

This friendliness to all manner of food preference may be one of the reasons there are fewer 100 percent vegetarian restaurants than you might expect in the Bay Area. There have been many closures in recent years and most have not been replaced by eateries with similar philosophies. In addition, many previously vegetarian restaurants have added meats, poultry, and seafood to their selections. The Bay Area is a tolerant place and there is more focus on organic, sustainable, and humanely raised products than on strict vegetarianism.

Any book, including this one, is shaped to some degree by the beliefs and biases of its author. I am not a vegetarian, though I have friends and relatives who practice virtually every form of diet, from standard vegetarian, vegan, and raw vegan to lacto-ovo-vegetarian, pesco-vegetarian, baco-vegetarian ("Bacon is not meat," I have been told in all seriousness, "it is fat."), and dedicated carnivore. I am an omnivore. As a restaurant critic for fifteen years, I was never willing to limit the scope of my work by excluding a category of potential deliciousness. That said, I understand and respect the vegetarian diet. However, I do feel that the communion of the table, the warmth and conversation and humanity we share when we dine together, is at least as important as what we eat and should not be forgotten when we dine with those with dietary philosophies different from our own. I believe, too, that our farmers and ranchers and fisherman and cheesemakers and cooks are present at our table; thus, I make an effort to find sustainably produced foods at restaurants where employees are treated well. I do not frequent fast-food chains and am one of those rare folks who has never eaten at McDonald's. I would never ridicule the choices of someone who shares a table with me, and I understand that if I am dining out with a vegan, it is best to try to find a vegan restaurant.

Finally, the visits for this book were conducted anonymously and we accepted no free meals, practices that I believe are mandatory for accurate restaurant evaluation.

ACKNOWLEDGMENTS

I am deeply grateful to Evelyn Cheatham, a remarkable chef, a vegetarian for nearly thirty years, and a dear friend, for her unwavering support and wisdom. Thanks, too, to Betty Ellsworth, a lifelong vegetarian, who provided invaluable technical support on this book. I also must thank Frédérique Lavoipierre, Nancy Lorenz, Susan Martin, Robin Pressmam, Katie Stohlman and David Browne for putting up with my complaining. And to Joanne Derbort, my editor at *The Press Democrat*, a huge hug of gratitude for sharing so much warmth and wisdom. Finally, an enormous thank you goes to my agent, Amy Rennert, for dealing with difficult situations with clarity, grace, and strength.

This book is dedicated to Patricia Ann Kewley, my dear friend whose all-too-short life ended as I worked on the manuscript.

About This Book

This guide is straightforward and easy to use. Each restaurant entry has a rating for food and cost, and a description of the atmosphere. It also includes a review and other pertinent information such as hours and types of payment accepted. Food and cost rating keys are listed below.

Food in each restaurant is rated as follows:

★	Fair
★★	Good
★★★	Excellent
★★★★	Outstanding

Cost for each restaurant is rated as follows:

$	Inexpensive (under $10)
$$	Moderate ($10 to $20)
$$$	Expensive ($21 and above)

The cost includes the price for an entrée, plus one drink and tip.

For the purposes of this guide, *vegetarian* means food that is prepared without any meat products. *Vegan* means food prepared without meat or dairy products. A note at the bottom of each restaurant listing indicates what kind of food is served in the restaurant. Not every restaurant in the book is strictly vegetarian. Some restaurants with full menus were also included if the vegetarian offerings were ample or if the restaurants were veg-friendly.

Restaurants

Alameda County

★★ / $

1. Krishna Restaurant

40645 Fremont Boulevard (near Grimmer Street)
Fremont, CA
510.656.2336

INDIAN

Hours:	Tue-Sun 11:00 a.m. to 8:00 p.m.
Payment:	Credit cards (no AmEx)
Parking:	Easy street parking
Atmosphere:	Casual

Formerly Manju Farsan House, it is still listed as such on many websites and in many guides, perhaps because the phone number remains the same and those who answer it tend not to have a working command of English. The food is classic Indian vegan cuisine without garlic and onions, a style common in the Gujarati region of India. Although there is full service here, takeout is even more popular. Gujarati sweets and snacks are a specialty.

VEGAN

★★ / $

2. Udupi Palace

5988 New Park Mall Road (near Cedar Boulevard)
Newark, CA
510.794.8400

SOUTH INDIAN

Hours:	*Mon-Th 11:00 a.m. to 10:00 p.m.*
	Fri-Sun 11:30 a.m. to 11:00 p.m.
Payment:	*Credit cards (no AmEx)*
Parking:	*Free lot*
Atmosphere:	*Casual*

Dosas—think spicy Indian crepes—are a signature
at this popular place that now has three locations
(Newark, Berkeley, and Sunnyvale). You can make
a meal simply of dosas, as many people do; there
is plenty of variety and they are delicious and satisfying. For a more diverse experience, Udupi
Palace offers a special combo meal with daal, two
curries, biryani, raita, chutney, rice pudding,
papadam, and steamed white rice cake; it's the
perfect way to go when you don't feel like thinking. There's mango lassi, and if you've ever been to
India, you'll be thrilled by the coffee, which
appears to be Nescafe in hot milk, a ubiquitous
beverage at cafes on the subcontinent.

VEGETARIAN

Berkeley and Oakland

★★/$
1. Ashkenaz Community Center

1317 San Pablo Avenue (near Gilman Avenue)
Berkeley, CA
510.525.5054

INTERNATIONAL

Hours:	*Open during Music Hall events,*
	Tue-Sun for late-evening events
Payment:	*Cash*
Parking:	*Easy*
Atmosphere:	*Dance Hall*

You don't go to Ashkenaz for dinner; you go for the music and the dancing and the other festive events and enjoy the fact that you can get dinner while you're at it. The owner is a committed vegetarian and includes many vegan options on his menus, which are offered only when there's something happening at this Berkeley landmark.

VEGETARIAN

★★/$$
2. Breads of India & Gourmet Curries

2448 Sacramento Street (near Dwight Way)
Berkeley, CA
510.848.7684

INDIAN

Hours:	*Daily 11:30 a.m. to 2:30 p.m.,*
	5:30 p.m. to 9:30 p.m.
Payment:	*Cash only*
Parking:	*Difficult street parking*
Atmosphere:	*Mid-scale casual*

With its big scarlet awning, Breads of India is easy to spot. Inside, the cuisine is as beautiful as that awning, with flavorful vegetable curries rotating daily. You'll find the usual Indian meat dishes—tandoori chicken, lamb curry—but the vegetable dishes receive the same loving preparation. And unlike many of the Indian restaurants in the Bay Area that focus on vegetarian preparations, Breads of India uses onions and garlic, which add layers of flavor that cannot be replaced by all the spices in the world. Diwani handi is a perfect example: a veritable garden of fresh vegetables is cooked in a thick sauce redolent with red onions and garlic accented by ginger and fennugreek leaves; it is outstanding. Khumbi da saag features whole mushrooms with spinach, onions, and a double rainbow of fragrant spices. Chickpea and spinach dumplings napped in a sauce based on buttermilk are both unusual and scrumptious.

VEGETARIAN FRIENDLY

★★★/$$
3. Cafe Fanny

1603 San Pablo Avenue (at Cedar Street)
Berkeley, CA
510.526.7664

CASUAL CALIFORNIAN

Hours:	*Mon-Fri 7:00 a.m. to 3:00 p.m.,*
	Sat 8:00 a.m. to 4:00 p.m.
	Sun 8:00 a.m. to 3:00 p.m.
Payment:	*Credit cards (no AmEx)*
Parking:	*Small free lot*
Atmosphere:	*French-style cafe with limited seating*

The casual sister cafe of Chez Panisse, Cafe Fanny is every bit as devoted to quality, freshness, and organics as Alice Waters' other endeavors. Cafe Fanny is famous for its granola, but try the egg dishes. They are as good as they are simple; poached eggs on levain with vinegar and oregano is extraordinary. At lunch, you won't go wrong with baked goat cheese with garden lettuces and toast; grilled mozzarella and tapenade on pain de mie; eggplant and fontina with red pepper puree, tapenade, and aioli on a sweet baguette; or egg salad (hold the anchovies) with sun-dried tomatoes. There's no better cafe latté—served in bowls—anywhere. There are great teas, and there are beignets, those gloriously delicious French doughnuts made famous in New Orleans. A plus is the location: Cafe Fanny is nestled between Kermit Lynch Wine Merchant and the original Acme Bakery.

VEGETARIAN FRIENDLY

★★★/$$$
4. Cha-Ya

1686 Shattuck Avenue (near Virginia Street)
Berkeley, CA
510.981.1213

JAPANESE

Hours:	*Tue-Sun 5:00 p.m. to 9:30 p.m.*
	Closed Mon
Payment:	*Credit cards (no AmEx)*
Parking:	*Free lot behind restaurant*
Atmosphere:	*Elegant, upscale*

If you don't arrive by 6:00 p.m. or so, expect a long wait at this extremely popular eatery, which does not take reservations. The kitchen creates classic dishes without the use of seaweed stock made with bonito flakes, generally ubiquitous in Japanese cooking. Among the best selections are udon and soba noodles with seaweed, mushrooms, and pristine vegetables; shredded vegetable salads with soybeans; innovative nigiri sushi; and extraordinary tempura. Cha-Ya is probably the best place in the Bay Area for a meal that is both traditionally Japanese and vegan.

VEGAN

★★★/$
5. The Cheese Board Pizza Collective

1512 Shattuck Avenue (near Vine Street)
Berkeley, CA
510.549.3055

PIZZA

Hours:	*Mon 11:30 a.m. to 2:00 p.m.*
	Tue-Fri 11:30 a.m. to 2:00 p.m.,
	4:30 p.m. to 7:00 p.m.
	Sat noon to 3:00 p.m.,
	4:30 p.m. to 7:00 p.m.
Payment:	*Cash only*
Parking:	*Moderately difficult street parking*
Atmosphere:	*Very casual*

In 1967, Elizabeth and Sahag Avedesian opened a little shop that would soon become an enduring Berkeley institution: the Cheese Board Collective. To achieve their goals of community, the Avedesians soon retooled their business so that it was a collective, with all workers sharing equally in every aspect of the business, a concept based on their experiences on an Israeli kibbutz. They have been supremely successful. In 1990, several members of the collective formed the Cheese Board Pizza Collective and began offering the delicious pizzas that the original collective had begun making. The pizzas are excellent, the atmosphere engaging and interesting.

VEGETARIAN FRIENDLY

★★★★/$$$
6. Chez Panisse Cafe

1517 Shattuck Avenue (near Cedar Street)
Berkeley, CA
510.548.5049

CALIFORNIA-FRENCH

Hours:	*Mon-Th 11:30 a.m. to 3:00 p.m.,*
	5:00 p.m. to 10:30 p.m.
	Fri-Sat 11:30 a.m. to 3:30 p.m.,
	5:00 p.m. to 11:30 p.m.
	Closed Sun
Payment:	*Credit cards*
Parking:	*Difficult street parking*
Atmosphere:	*Upscale, lively*

Chez Panisse remains the benchmark for fresh,
local, and organic foods. Alice Waters' unwaver-
ing commitment to these concepts is reason
enough for any vegetarian to enjoy a meal here.
There is always at least one vegetarian appetizer
and one vegetarian entrée, and the staff is
happy to adjust items to suit vegan require-
ments, too. (Downstairs, with its prix fixe
menu, is more difficult, especially for vegans,
but if you do find yourself dining downstairs,
they will accommodate you.) Upstairs is livelier
and less expensive, and the menu, which
changes frequently, offers many enticing choices.
Pizzas, from the wood-fired oven, are outstand-
ing. Anything with peaches is a good bet, as
Waters has a unique passion for the stone fruit
and serves them only at their perfect moment of
ripeness. The garden salad with chevre and crou-
tons launched a culinary revolution.

VEGETARIAN FRIENDLY

★★/$

7. Crepevine

5600 College Avenue (near Ocean View)
Oakland, CA
510.658.2026

MIDDLE EASTERN CREPERY

Hours:	*Sun-Th 7:30 a.m. to 11:00 p.m.*
	Fri-Sat 7:30 a.m. to midnight
Payment:	*Cash and local checks only*
Parking:	*Difficult street parking during peak hours*
Atmosphere:	*Very casual, lively (counter service)*

This place is often mistakenly identified as a vegetarian restaurant, but it isn't. You'll find poultry, beef, pork, and seafood among the selections. There are, however, plenty of choices for both vegans and vegetarians. In addition to fairly standard California-Mediterranean sandwiches, salads, and pastas, there are about a dozen egg dishes, a tofu scramble with mushrooms and spinach, and a lot of crepes. For crepes, we like Le Delice (cheddar cheese with glazed onions) and Greek (spinach, olives, almonds, onions, and feta cheese with cucumber yogurt sauce). Sweet crepes include one with Nutella and bananas. You can, if you prefer, create your own combinations. Anyone for Nutella and tofu?

VEGETARIAN FRIENDLY

★★/$
8. Eat-A-Pita

2511 Durant Avenue (near Telegraph Avenue)
Berkeley, CA
510.841.6482

MIDDLE EASTERN

Hours:	*Daily 10:30 a.m. to 10:00 p.m.*
Payment:	*Credit cards (no AmEx)*
Parking:	*Difficult street parking*
Atmosphere:	*Casual*

Here you'll find classic Middle Eastern selections
such as hummus, baba ganoush, tabbouleh,
fried eggplant, marinated vegetables, and generous salads and sandwiches. Khiar yogurt salad
with cucumbers and mint is particularly appeal-
ing, as is a rice and lentil plate.

VEGETARIAN FRIENDLY

★★/$
9. Ethiopia Restaurant

2955 Telegraph Avenue (near Ashby Avenue)
Berkeley, CA
510.843.1992

ETHIOPIAN

Hours:	*Daily 11:30 a.m. to 11:00 p.m.*
Payment:	*Credit cards*
Parking:	*Moderate street parking*
Atmosphere:	*Mid-scale casual, patio dining*

Although you'll find beef, lamb, poultry, and shrimp here, the menu boasts that there are 792 vegetarian combinations available, a function more of math than of diversity. A combination plate offering a choice of five vegetarian dishes from among twelve selections offers that many variations. However, the selections themselves are both unfamiliar to most Americans and delicious. Cold potato porridge, hot and spicy green lentil salad, collard greens, mushroom stew, bulgur, lentil-stuffed samboussas, and green peppers with sunflower seed juice are among the selections that offer a feast for both vegetarians and vegans.

VEGETARIAN FRIENDLY

★★/$$
10. Golden Lotus Vegetarian Restaurant

1301 Franklin Street (near 13th Street)
Oakland, CA
510.893.0383

VIETNAMESE & CHINESE

Hours:	*Mon-Th 10:00 a.m. to 9:00 p.m.*
	Fri-Sat 10:00 a.m. to 10:00 p.m.
	Sun 11:00 a.m. to 9:00 p.m.
Payment:	*Credit cards (no AmEx)*
Parking:	*Moderately difficult street parking*
Atmosphere:	*Casual, urban-diner style*

Many regular customers boast that Golden Lotus offers the best faux meat dishes around. The flavors of the pho (traditionally made with beef) are bold and true, fried Imperial rolls are excellent, sauteed garlic "beef" draws raves, and even clay pot "fish" offers more than mere compromise. Nearly everything here is vegan and it is easy to spot what isn't. Service is hit and miss, but the food is good enough that you should turn on your patience switch and smile as much as you can.

MOSTLY VEGAN

★★/$
11. Juice Bar Collective

2114 Vine Street (near Shattuck Avenue)
Berkeley, CA
510. 548.8473

AMERICAN

Hours:	Mon-Sat 10:00 a.m. to 4:30 p.m. Closed Sun
Payment:	Cash, traveler's checks, local checks
Parking:	Difficult street parking
Atmosphere:	Very casual juice bar, outside tables

With the exception of turkey and tuna, all the offerings here are vegetarian. For an excellent contrast in taste and texture, try polenta pizza and cabbage salad, or Thai cucumber salad with lentil loaf burger. If you need to feed your inner child, there's macaroni and cheese, chocolate chip cookies, and banana smoothies. For dessert, how can you resist sweet potato pie? For fifty cents, you can add fresh ginger to any of the house-made juices; it is particularly good in the carrot juice.

MOSTLY VEGETARIAN

★/$
12. Long Life Vegi House

2129 University Avenue (near Shattuck Avenue)
Berkeley, CA
510.845.6072

CHINESE

Hours:	Mon-Fri 11:30 a.m. to 10:00 p.m.
	Sat-Sun 11:30 a.m. to 10:30 p.m.
Payment:	Credit cards
Parking:	Difficult street parking
Atmosphere:	Casual, Asian eclectic

Vegetarian selections share equal space with seafood selections here. There is a large selection of faux meats as well, including vegi-ham, vegi-chicken, vegi-beef, and vegi-pork. Garlicky mixed nuts, noodles with spicy bean sauce, tan-tan noodles, Chinese greens with black mushrooms, and a sizzling tofu platter with black mushrooms and carrots are among the best selections.

VEGETARIAN FRIENDLY

★★/$$
13. Meant to Be Music

2120 Allston Way (at Shattuck Avenue)
Berkeley, CA
510.841.2662

INTERNATIONAL

Hours:	Tue-Sun 5:00 p.m. to 1:00 a.m.
	Closed Mon
Payment:	Credit cards
Parking:	Difficult street parking,
	public lots nearby
Atmosphere:	Lively, eclectic

Formerly Anna's Bistro, this is a place with a mission: to foster and perhaps even create community. To that end, all are welcome here, from committed carnivores to vegans, who sometimes even nestle next to each other in the comfy overstuffed velvet sofas. There's music every night, board games, and lively conversation among strangers. The ever-changing menu may feature vegan black bean soup, curried pumpkin soup, artichokes stuffed with blue cheese, vegetarian three-bean chile, and Colombian corn pancakes with shredded cabbage and chipotle-scented sour cream. The politically astute will enjoy the menu's notation that Larry Bensky, the acclaimed radio journalist (and a longtime vegetarian) who is a fixture at nearby KPFA-FM, has selected several of the wines for the wine list.

VEGETARIAN FRIENDLY

★★★/$$
14. Nan Yang Rockridge

6048 College Avenue (near Claremont Avenue)
Oakland, CA
510.655.3298

BURMESE

Hours:	*Tue-Fri 11:30 a.m. to 3:00 p.m.,*
	5:00 p.m. to 10:00 p.m.
	Sat 11:30 a.m. to 10:00 p.m.
	Sun noon to 9:30 p.m.
	Closed Mon
Payment:	*Credit cards (no AmEx)*
Parking:	*Easy to moderately difficult street parking*
Atmosphere:	*Clean, bright, mid-scale*

Based on what visitors to Burma have to say about its cuisine, you might find the quality and creativity here surprising. The food is unfamiliar to the American palate but it is not challenging, as some unfamiliar cuisines can be. Garlic noodles with spinach and tomatoes, and elaborate salads with layers of flavor and contrasting textures are delightful. Not everything is vegetarian, but the majority of dishes are. There are options for vegans, too.

VEGETARIAN FRIENDLY

★/$$
15. New World Vegetarian

464 8th Street (near Broadway)
Oakland, CA
510.444.2891

INTERNATIONAL

Hours:	Mon-Fri 11:00 a.m. to 3:00 p.m., 5:00 p.m. to 9:30 p.m.
	Sat 11:00 a.m. to 9:30 p.m.
	Sun 11:00 a.m. to 9:00 p.m.
Payment:	Credit cards (no AmEx)
Parking:	Moderately difficult street parking, public lot across street
Atmosphere:	Clean, bright, mid-scale

You'll find a veritable feast of faux meat dishes here, from barbecued "pork" to crispy "fish" and "pork" sausages. They are presented as longtime favorites like chicken cacciatore and pepper steak and as innovative signature dishes. If you prefer things that look like vegetables and beans, try the okra and bean stew, the three-bean stew, seaweed tofu soup, or creamy soy onions. Clay pot dishes are good, too. This place may not be the best choice for omnivores or mainstream vegetarians but activist vegans will love it.

VEGETARIAN

★★★/$

16. OlivetoDownstairs & Cafe

5655 College Avenue (at Shafter Avenue)
Oakland, CA
510.547.5356

ITALIAN

Hours:	Mon 7:00 a.m. to 9:00 p.m.
	Tue-Wed 7:00 a.m. to 9:30 p.m.
	Thu-Fri 7:00 a.m. to 10:00 p.m.
	Sat 8:00 a.m. to 10:00 p.m.
	Sun 8:00 a.m. to 9:00 p.m.
Payment:	Credit cards
Parking:	Moderately difficult street parking and small lot
Atmosphere:	Rustic

In the heart of upscale Rockridge, Oliveto-Downstairs is accessible, affordable, and delicious, with a classic Italian trattoria atmosphere. At breakfast, you'll find polenta with cream and poached fruit, toast with poached fruit, breakfast pizzas, and house-made granola. At lunch there are yummy small plates (fennel salad, red cabbage with walnuts and Parmigiano-Reggiano) and big sandwiches. In the evenings, foods from the brick oven—thin-crusted pizzas, baked pastas, and lots of specials—are a focus. There is plenty of pancetta and prosciutto here, so be sure to ask if you aren't sure that a dish is vegetarian. Oliveto offers an outstanding selection of premium teas, available anytime. Upstairs, Oliveto Restaurant is open for lunch and dinner and is considered one of the best restaurants in the Bay Area. It is not, however, as vegetarian friendly as downstairs.

VEGETARIAN FRIENDLY

★★/$
17. Organic Cafe & Macrobiotic Market

1050 40th Street (near Market Street)
Oakland, CA
510.653.6510

Macrobiotic

Hours:	*Daily 9:00 a.m. to 9:00 p.m.*
Payment:	*Credit cards*
Parking:	*Moderately difficult street parking*
Atmosphere:	*In-store cafe, buffet*

There is no printed menu here, just notations on a blackboard that change daily. Nearly everything is organic, most of it is vegan, and it's all very inexpensive, making it popular with students and the local art community who flock to the daily lunch buffet. Expect a lot of legumes—beans, lentils, and peas—and greens, paired in interesting, delicious, and healthy ways.

Organic and Macrobiotic Vegetarian

★★/$
18. Raw Energy Organic Juice Cafe

2050 Addison Street (near Shattuck Avenue)
Berkeley, CA
510.665.9464

RAW ORGANIC

Hours:	*Mon-Fri 8:30 a.m. to 6:30 p.m.*
	Sat noon to 4:00 p.m.
	Closed Sun
Payment:	*Credit cards (no AmEx)*
Parking:	*Difficult street parking,*
	public lot nearby
Atmosphere:	*Very casual juice bar*

Here's a place that is extremely friendly to any-one with food issues. A detailed menu puts most concerns to rest: fruits and vegetables are not only from local organic farmers, they are also harvested at perfect ripeness and delivered within a day or two; the potent garlic leaves will not make your breath smell; and both the wheat grass and barley grass will oxygenate your cells and give you a buzz and a burst of energy. Single juices are delicious (we love the watermelon) and the blends are bright and interesting, with something for everyone. The food menu offers pizza (with a raw sprouted-nut crust), several salads, an excellent veggie sand-wich, crackers, soup, and several desserts.

ORGANIC RAW VEGETARIAN

★★/$
19. Razan's Kitchen

2119 Kittredge Street (near Fulton)
Berkeley, CA
510.486.0449

INTERNATIONAL ORGANIC

Hours:	Daily 10:00 a.m. to 10:00 p.m.
Payment:	Credit cards
Parking:	Easy street parking and free lot
Atmosphere:	Casual, lively

The emphasis here is not on vegetarian fare but on conscientious cuisine, whether from animal sources or not. Nearly everything is organic; poultry, meat, and seafood are from respectable sources; and vegetables are fresh, bright, and beautifully prepared in salads, sandwiches, burritos, and platters. A garden burrito, a mushroom saute, and fresh juices are among the selections most popular with students from the nearby UC Berkeley campus.

VEGETARIAN FRIENDLY

★★/$
20. Smart Alec's Intelligent Food

2355 Telegraph Avenue (near Durant)
Berkeley, CA
510.704.4000

AMERICAN

Hours:	Daily 11:00 a.m. to 9:00 p.m.
Payment:	Cash, traveler's checks, local checks
Parking:	Difficult street parking
Atmosphere:	Casual fast food

Vegetarian purists might quibble with the burgers, chicken, tuna, and turkey on the menu, but there are so many good vegetable selections here, including homemade soups, that it's impossible to dismiss Smart Alec's. Try the Garden Delight salad, with wheat berries, fresh soybeans, garbanzos, and corn added to a standard tossed salad; sesame vinaigrette is the perfect dressing. An eggplant melt sandwich, a hummus sandwich, and vegan chili with cheese and green onion are also quite good.

VEGETARIAN FRIENDLY

★★/$$
21. A Taste of Africa

3031 Adeline Street (near Ashby Avenue)
Berkeley, CA
510.843.6316

WEST AFRICAN

Hours:	*Tue-Sat 1:00 p.m. to 8:00 p.m.*
	Closed Sun-Mon
	Sat-Sun (at the Ashby Flea Market)
	11:00 a.m. to 6:00 p.m.
Payment:	*Credit cards (no AmEx)*
Parking:	*Moderate street parking, free lot*
Atmosphere:	*Rustic*

Although the West African diet generally includes substantial quantities of meat, this charmingly homey cafe has plenty to offer the vegetarian. Spinach with peanuts, rice with vegetables and a creamy peanut sauce, and flat bread made of corn flour are among the vegetarian-friendly dishes. Although this little space is designed primarily for catering and take-out food, there are a few tables and plenty of warm hospitality. If you love fiery fare, be sure to ask for the hot sauce; it will challenge even the most jaded palates.

VEGETARIAN FRIENDLY

★★/$

22. Udupi Palace

1901 University Avenue
(at Martin Luther King Jr. Way)
Berkeley, CA
510.843.6600

SOUTH INDIAN

Hours:	*Daily 9:00 a.m. to 10:00 p.m.*
Payment:	*Cash only*
Parking:	*Difficult street parking*
Atmosphere:	*Casual, family-friendly*

Dosas—think spicy Indian crepes—are a signature
at this popular place that now has three locations
(Newark, Berkeley, and Sunnyvale). You can make
a meal simply of dosas, as many people do; there
is plenty of variety and they are delicious and satisfying. For a more diverse experience, Udupi
Palace offers a special combo meal with daal, two
curries, biryani, raita, chutney, rice pudding,
papadam, and steamed white rice cake; it's the
perfect way to go when you don't feel like thinking. There's mango lassi, and if you've ever been to
India, you'll be thrilled by the coffee, which
appears to be Nescafe in hot milk, a ubiquitous
beverage at cafes on the subcontinent.

VEGETARIAN

★★/$
23. Vege House

369 12th Street
  (near Lincoln Neighborhood Center and Broadway)
Oakland, CA
510.465.4713

CHINESE & VIETNAMESE

Hours:	Mon-Thu 9:00 a.m. to 7:00 p.m.
	Fri-Sun 9:00 a.m. to 6:30 p.m.
Payment:	Cash only
Parking:	Difficult street parking
Atmosphere:	Casual, lively

There is a trend in many parts of the Bay Area to combine Chinese and Vietnamese cuisines in a single restaurant, and that is the case with the two Vege House locations, here and in San Francisco (see page 110). Among the specialties are excellent fried tofu—good with spicy chili sauce. The menu includes copious quantities of mock meats, as well.

VEGETARIAN

★★/$
24. Vegi Food

2085 Vine Street (near Shattuck Avenue)
Berkeley, CA
510.548.5244

CHINESE

Hours:	Mon 5:00 p.m. to 9:00 p.m.
	Tue-Fri 11:30 a.m. to 3:00 p.m.,
	5:00 p.m. to 9:00 p.m.
	Sat-Sun 11:30 a.m. to 9:00 p.m.
Payment:	Cash and local checks only
Parking:	Difficult street parking
Atmosphere:	Casual, quiet, friendly

The name leaves no doubt about the food served
in this little Chinese restaurant. Not only is
there no meat or seafood anywhere on the
premises, the kitchen uses no eggs, garlic,
onions, or MSG. Instead, you'll find a mix of
mock meat and fresh vegetables in such familiar
dishes as chow mein, pot stickers, spring rolls,
fried rice, and stir-fries. We particularly enjoyed
the spicy cabbage with black mushrooms, straw
mushrooms with snow peas, and fried walnuts
with sweet-and-sour sauce. Several of the dishes
are very spicy.

VEGETARIAN

★★/$$
25. Vik's Chaat Corner

726 Allston Way (near 4th Street)
Berkeley, CA
510.644.4412

INDIAN SNACK SHOP

Hours:	*Tue-Sun 11:00 a.m. to 6:00 p.m.*
	Closed Mon
Payment:	*Credit cards (no AmEx)*
Parking:	*Free lot*
Atmosphere:	*Large, trendy, kid-friendly*

One of the best signs in any ethnic restaurant is the presence of native diners, and you'll find plenty of Indian families enjoying a meal at this industrial-style eatery. A chaat is a snack and there are a bounty of them here, from golden samosas filled with peas and potatoes to pooris as light and airy as a cumulus cloud. Chutneys and sauces of fresh mint and cilantro add the perfect contrast. Not everything is vegetarian, so if you aren't sure about something, don't be afraid to ask. (And for all manner of Indian supplies, stop at nearby Vik's Distributing, one of the best Indian supermarkets around.)

VEGETARIAN FRIENDLY

Marin County

★★/$$
1. Caffe Oggi

745 East Blithedale Avenue (near Camino Alto)
Mill Valley, CA
415.383.4355

ITALIAN

Hours:	Mon-Fri 7:00 a.m. to 6:00 p.m.
	Sat 8:00 a.m. to 3:00 p.m.
	Closed Sun
Payment:	Credit cards
Parking:	Large free lot
Atmosphere:	Casual cafe, outdoor tables

Caffe Oggi is a great place for take-out vegetarian meals. Sliced carrots are sweet and succulent, spinach in garlic is outstanding, Swiss chard bursts with freshness, and broccoli with cauliflower is both beautiful and delicious. Vegetable pastas are good, too, and a complex timpano made with spaghetti, penne, farfalle, pasta shells, zucchini, cheese, and tomato sauce is so good that it almost defies description. Gnocchi (potato dumplings) are good, too, and at lunch there's a decent selection of vegetable panini. Don't bother with the dull Caesar salad. Service often borders on rude and dismissive, so you might want to drink an espresso before placing your order, as the added energy will help you break through the odd distance of the staff.

VEGETARIAN FRIENDLY

★★★★/$$$
2. Fork

198 Sir Francis Drake Boulevard
  (at Tunstead Avenue)
San Anselmo, CA
415.453.9898

CALIFORNIA-FRENCH

Hours:	Tue-Sat 11:45 a.m. to 2:30 p.m.
	5:30 p.m. to 9:30 p.m.
	Closed Sun-Mon
Payment:	Credit cards
Parking:	Moderate street parking, small free lot
Atmosphere:	Elegant, lively

Fork is another ideal example of the ease with which vegetarians can dine anywhere in the Bay Area. There is always a vegetarian tasting menu (selections change daily), though this is not the sort of place where you'll find faux meats. Instead, you'll find such delights as cauliflower gratin with glazed carrots and horseradish; radicchio and frisee with almonds, oranges, and local blue cheese; braised endive with fingerling potatoes and matsutake mushroom risotto. Soups—carrot broth with chervil sabayon, celery root with apple chutney and walnut oil—are glorious, and a side of potato puree with truffle oil and chives is the stuff of dreams. At lunch a grilled cheese sandwich made on brioche with white cheddar cheese, and house-made tomato soup alongside, is outstanding. Fork serves small plates, little portions that allow you to eat lightly and try several different things. Kitchen techniques are flawless and ingredients celebrate the bounty of local producers. Host and co-owner, Charlie Low, and executive chef, Scott Howard, are warm and gracious and will answer any questions you have about the selections.

VEGETARIAN FRIENDLY

★★★★/$
3. Green Gulch Farm

Shoreline Highway
  (between Mill Valley and Stinson Beach)
Stinson Beach, CA
415.383.3134

VEGETARIAN

Hours:	Sun 12:45 p.m. (single lunch seating and no established closing time)
Payment:	$8 suggested donation
Parking:	On-site, free for cars of three or more, otherwise $5
Atmosphere:	Peaceful, quiet, spectacular location

Each Sunday, the San Francisco Zen Center's Green Gulch Farm is open to the public, with meditation instruction beginning at 8:15 a.m., a lecture at 10:15 a.m., tea at 11:15 a.m., and lunch, open to the public, at 12:45 p.m. This serene setting is one of the Bay Area's jewels. Consult the Zen center's website—www.sfzc.com—for other special and ongoing events, including the practice of tea, that are open to the public.

VEGETARIAN

★★/$$
4. India Village

555 East Francisco Boulevard (near Bellam Way)
San Rafael, CA
415.456.2411

INDIAN

Hours:	Mon-Sat 11:30 a.m. to 2:30 p.m.,
	5:00 p.m. to 9:30 p.m.
	Sun 5:00 p.m. to 9:00 p.m.
Payment:	Credit cards
Parking:	Easy street parking
Atmosphere:	Rustic

India Village is nestled in among car dealerships, furniture stores, and repair shops along the canal in eastern San Rafael, but its decor suggests exactly what its name implies—an Indian village. The naan here is outstanding, especially the harabara naan, which is slathered with a puree of cilantro and mint. Vegetable samosas with a dense mixture of potato, onion, spinach, and fragrant spices are good, too, and an unusual spinach leaf pakora is sublime, with pert spinach leaves that somehow hold up to the garbanzo batter and the deep frying. Vegetable biryani is often too moist and full of big chunks of vegetables, but Kashmiri pilau (basmati rice with peas) is light and delicate. Be sure to order raita and chutney, both necessary condiments with Indian fare.

VEGETARIAN FRIENDLY

★★★/$
5. Jhan Thong

5835 Northgate Mall (at the Terra Linda exit)
San Rafael, CA
415.499.3501

THAI

Hours:	*Mon-Sat 11:00 a.m. to 9:00 p.m.*
	Sun 11:00 a.m. to 6:00 p.m.
Payment:	*Cash only*
Parking:	*Large free lot*
Atmosphere:	*Food mall*

Traffic in the North Bay can be so bad that it's handy to know of eateries near the 101 corridor in case there's a lengthy backup. Jhan Thong is just the sort of place to save the day. In the food court of a large generic mall, it is far superior to what its location suggests. Bameeyam, a salad of egg noodles, julienned vegetables, and sesame dressing, is light and refreshing; tofu in green curry is excellent; and eggplant in black bean sauce couldn't be better. But an unusual version of mee krob, a traditional Thai salad, may be the star here—crisp, thin noodles are tossed with crispy tofu, vegetables, ginger, lime, cilantro, coconut, and peanuts for spectacular results. There are a lot of beef, seafood, and poultry items here, too, so you'll need to navigate the day's choices and ask if you aren't sure.

VEGETARIAN FRIENDLY

★★★/$$
6. Lotus

704 Fourth Street (near Lincoln Avenue)
San Rafael, CA
415.456.5808

INDIAN

Hours:	Mon-Sat 11:30 a.m. to 2:30 p.m.,
	5:00 p.m. to 9:30 p.m.
	Sun 5:00 p.m. to 9:00 p.m.
Payment:	Credit cards
Parking:	Easy street parking
Atmosphere:	Elegant, mid-scale

Regardless of what else you may order here, be sure to get channe ki chaat, an appetizer of tender chickpeas, potatoes, and onions with yogurt and a slightly sweet tamarind sauce. It is much more than the sum of its parts; it is sublime. Paired with garlic or onion naan, it can be a complete meal in itself. Yet there are other good dishes for vegetarians, including delicately seasoned daal, excellent vegetable biryani, and, for dessert, kheer, a lovely chilled rice pudding that includes black pepper among its many spices. Both versions of lassi—one scented with rose water, the other made with mango—are excellent, and the chai here puts the ubiquitous commercial versions to shame. A wine list offers excellent selections that suit the cuisine.

VEGETARIAN FRIENDLY

7. Lydia's Lovin' Food

31 Bolinas Road (at Mono Avenue)
Fairfax, CA
415.456.5300

INTERNATIONAL

Hours:	Mon-Thu 8:00 a.m. to 10:00 p.m.
	Fri-Sun 10:00 a.m. to 11:00 p.m.
Payment:	Credit cards
Parking:	Moderately difficult street parking
Atmosphere:	Eclectic

At press time for this guide, Lydia's Lovin' Foods was under construction, preparing for a mid-spring opening. The menu is divided between "Live" and "Cooked" offerings, with raw dishes making up the bulk of the selections. Crackers, pizza crusts, and croquettes are made with sprouted nuts and seeds; nuts are employed in other dishes, too, such as savory cream sauces and sweet frostings. There are several salads, including garlic, dulse, and sesame in shallot vinaigrette and 7 Sprout Delight. The cooked menu includes black bean dip, corn salad, squash and kale soup, polenta with vegetables, Thai noodles with eggplant and basil, and baked tofu with kale and sesame seeds. In addition to being a full-service restaurant, Lydia's is a community for vegetarians, and even has a stage for everything from poetry readings and story-telling to dance and puppet shows. There are education stations, a community dining table, a play area for kids, and books and binders full of information on a variety of issues, including food combining and alternative energy sources.

VEGAN

★★★/$$$
8. Parkside Cafe

43 Arenal Avenue (at Shoreline Highway)
Stinson Beach, CA
415.868.1272

CALIFORNIAN

Hours:	Mon-Fri 7:30 a.m. to 2:00 p.m.
	Sat-Sun 8:00 a.m. to 2:00 p.m.
	(breakfast)
	Daily 11:00 a.m. to 2:00 p.m.
	(lunch)
	Fri-Sun 2:00 p.m. to 5:00 p.m.
	(patio barbecue)
	Mon, Th-Sun 5:00 p.m. to 10:00 p.m.
	(take-out pizza)
	Mon, Th-Sun 5:00 p.m. to 10:00 p.m.
	(dinner)
Payment:	Credit cards
Parking:	Moderately difficult street parking, difficult during summer months
Atmosphere:	Casually elegant with a fireplace

Vegans with food issues will do well to avoid this outpost of fine dining, as the presence of foie gras likely will eclipse any potential enjoyment. But other vegetarians will find much to enjoy here. In the spring, a casserole of tiny pasta, asparagus, portobellos, and fresh fava beans is about as delicious and satisfying a dish as you'll find anywhere. On summer afternoons, barbecues on the patio include vegetable kabobs, and salads are always excellent. Do not be confused by the snack bar with its hot dogs and hamburgers. This is really three eateries in one and inside is where you'll find the coolest cuisine. Pizzas, available for takeout, are good, too, though fairly conventional.

VEGETARIAN FRIENDLY

★★★★/$$$
9. Roxanne's

320 Magnolia Avenue (near Monte Vista Avenue)
Larkspur, CA
415.924.5004

Raw Vegan

Hours:	Tue-Sun 5:30 p.m. to 10:00 p.m.
	Closed Mon
Payment:	Credit cards
Parking:	Free lot
Atmosphere:	Elegant

Roxanne's pristine cuisine caused a sensation from the moment the restaurant opened its sustainably built doors, though complaints about leaving the restaurant hungry soon followed. If you think of eating at Roxanne's as an experience instead of a mere meal, you'll delight in the small portions of exquisitely presented foods. Roxanne's location in the heart of Marin County is ideal. The cuisine is interesting, beautiful, and flavorful, with a substantial amount of richness wrought from unlikely ingredients. Smoked almond cheese, marinated cashew cheese, carrot soup with truffled sour cream, and yellow curry with creamy parsnips—all vegan and all prepared without heat—are among the selections on a fall menu. Roxanne and Michael Klein apply their philosophy to the entire endeavor, using not only organic foods but also nontoxic, recycled, or sustainable materials in the building as well as solar power from a system installed on the restaurant's roof. All of the restaurant's profits are donated to nonprofit organizations.

Raw vegan

★★★/$$
10. Roxanne's-To-Go

316 Magnolia Avenue
Larkspur, CA
415.924.5004

RAW VEGAN

Hours:	*Mon-Sat 10:00 a.m. to 8:00 p.m.*
	Sun 10:00 a.m. to 5:00 p.m.
Payment:	*Cash, credit cards*
Parking:	*Easy street parking*
Atmosphere:	*Takeout*

Roxanne's-To-Go, the take-out twin of Roxanne's, makes this philosophically driven raw cuisine more accessible to more people more often. You no longer have to set aside two to three hours to see what all the buzz is about. Selections include lasagne, dolmas, pad Thai, pizza, sea vegetable salad, bagels and cream cheese, empanadas, desserts, ice creams, juices, smoothies, supplements, and more, all of it organic, vegan, and raw—which is to say, never heated beyond 118 degrees. You'll also find cookbooks, cooking implements, and other materials relevant to raw food preparation and lifestyle.

RAW VEGAN

★★/$

11. Sher-e-Punjab

1025 C Street (between 4th and 5th Streets)
San Rafael, CA
415.459.1320

INDIAN

Hours:	*Mon-Sat 11:30 a.m. to 2:30 p.m.,*
	5:00 p.m. to 10:00 p.m.
	Closed Sun
Payment:	*Credit cards (no AmEx)*
Parking:	*Free public lot*
Atmosphere:	*Casual, mid-scale*

This sweet little place is nestled between a charming thrift shop and an Apple computer store. Servers are extremely gracious and friendly and the food is excellent. Although the salt lassi with rose water is a bit odd, mango lassi is the best we've had anywhere. Dal makhni, a curry of dark lentils in a rich sauce, is excellent, especially with a little raita alongside. Aloo gobhi with potatoes, cauliflower, and plenty of turmeric is luscious, and the naan are outstanding. Vegetarian pakoras are almost shockingly good. Biryani is served in a stainless-steel dish and inverted onto a platter tableside by a server; it is good but needs both chutney and raita to really come alive. A daily lunch buffet, a veritable groaning board, is just $6.95 and comes with piping hot naan.

VEGETARIAN FRIENDLY

Mendocino and Lake Counties

★★★/$
1. Junkang-Restaurant at City of 10,000 Buddhas

4951 Bodhi Way (near Highway 101)
Talmage (near Ukiah), CA
707.462.0939

VEGETARIAN

Hours:	Mon, Wed-Thu 11:00 a.m. to 3:00 p.m. (lunch only)
	Fri-Sun 11:00 a.m. to 6:00 p.m.
	Closed Tue
Payment:	Cash, traveler's checks, local checks
Parking:	Free lot
Atmosphere:	Quiet and dignified, gorgeous grounds

About two hours north of San Francisco is a conservative Buddhist monastery with a restaurant open to the public nearly every day. The food is fresh and pristine, completely vegetarian and mostly vegan, with no onions or garlic. You won't necessarily recognize—or like—everything, but it is always interesting and the serene environment adds a welcome respite from the busy world. The setting is beautiful, and as gently invigorating as the food.

VEGETARIAN

★★/$
2. Nature's Bounty

301 North Main (near 4th Street)
Lakeport, CA
707.263.4575

Californian

Hours:	*Mon-Th 10:00 a.m. to 3:00 p.m.*
	Fri-Sun 10:00 a.m. to 5:00 p.m.
Payment:	*Credit cards (no AmEx)*
Parking:	*Free lot*
Atmosphere:	*Casual, in-store deli*

Getting a decent meal, let alone a vegetarian meal, away from urban areas can be difficult, even in organic-minded California. This little outpost is an exception. You'll not only find excellent salads and fresh juices such as carrot, orange, and mixed vegetable, but also cheese made from sunflower seeds, wheat grass juice, cornmeal focaccia, and homemade soups. There are some interesting substitutions for ingredients not generally considered harmful. For instance, instead of pepper, which the menu claims is a stomach irritant, you'll find toasted cumin. In place of vinegar, too harsh for the stomach lining we are told, the kitchen uses lemon and lime juice. And instead of mustard—a stomach irritant? who knew?—you can have your salad, sandwich, or vegi burger smeared with roasted garlic. Most menu items list calories and grams of fat.

Vegan

★★★★/$$$

3. The Ravens Restaurant (at Stanford Inn by the Sea Bed and Breakfast and Spa)

Highway 1 and Comptche Ukiah Road
Mendocino, CA
800.331.8884

CALIFORNIAN

Hours:	Daily breakfast from 8:00 a.m.
	Nightly dinner from 5:30 p.m.
Payment:	Credit cards
Parking:	Free lot
Atmosphere:	Elegant, upscale

What a rare find The Ravens is, at this lovely inn and spa with its gorgeous gardens and beautiful llamas. (The restaurant is named for a pair of ravens who took up residence here.) Vegetarian fare is rarely featured in such indulgent surroundings. The quality, whether at breakfast or dinner, is outstanding, and you should simply let your inclinations guide you rather than use our recommendations, as the menu changes frequently and there is nary a misstep in the kitchen. A Caesar salad features crispy nori instead of anchovies; a salad with dark cherry vinaigrette, shaved fennel, and toasted pecans will dazzle any palate; and a plate of local mushrooms features some of the rarest fungi you'll ever see outside a forest. For breakfast, try the grilled citrus polenta with sautéed garden greens and cashew sauce.

VEGETARIAN

Napa and Contra Costa Counties

★★/$
1. Ambrosia Garden

834 San Pablo Avenue
  (between Solano and Washington)
Albany, CA
510.528.5388

Cantonese & Taiwanese

Hours:	*Sun-Th 11:30 a.m. to 9:30 p.m.*
	Fri-Sat 11:30 a.m. to 10:00 p.m.
	Closed Tue
Payment:	*Credit cards (no AmEx)*
Parking:	*Easy street parking*
Atmosphere:	*Bright, nicely appointed room*

You'll find classic Chinese fare here, including many vegetarian versions of familiar meat and seafood dishes, such as walnut "prawns," spicy kung pau "chicken," and "ants climbing up a tree," our favorite. The quality of both ingredients and preparation is consistently good. Service is generally warm and friendly, and the atmosphere is pleasantly relaxing.

Vegetarian

★★★/$$$
2. Bistro Don Giovanni

4110 St. Helena Highway (at Zinfandel Lane)
St. Helena, CA
707.224.3300

ITALIAN

Hours:	Sun-Th 11:30 a.m. to 9:30 p.m.
	Fri-Sat 11:30 a.m. to 10:00 p.m.
Payment:	Credit cards
Parking:	Large free lot
Atmosphere:	Noisy, bustling trattoria

Here's another example of the ease with which vegetarians can eat almost anywhere in the vast Bay Area. Although the menu is heavily meated, side dishes present outstanding options: Phipps (an organic farm on the central coast) beans in olive oil; sautéed spinach with lemon and garlic; brussels sprouts with brown butter, capers, and Parmigiano; and buttermilk mashed potatoes. Even the pickiest vegan could put together a good meal. In addition, there's an excellent plate of beets and tiny green beans served with avocado, fennel, and Roquefort vinaigrette; fried olives and almonds; greens with apples, persimmons, walnuts, and blue cheese; and pumpkin-filled pasta with sage brown butter. Remember that selections change seasonally; vegetarians should go straight to the "Contorni" section at the end of the menu.

VEGETARIAN FRIENDLY

★★★/$$
3. Ephesus Kebab Lounge

1321 Locust Street (at Mt. Diablo Boulevard)
Walnut Creek, CA
925.945.8082

TURKISH

Hours:	*Mon-Th 11:00 a.m. to 10:00 p.m.*
	Fri-Sat 11:00 a.m. to 11:00 p.m.
	Sun 4:30 p.m. to 10:00 p.m.
Payment:	*Credit cards*
Parking:	*Moderate street parking*
Atmosphere:	*Elegant, mid-scale, lively*

You don't immediately think of vegetables when you see the name of this place, as kabobs tend to be synonymous with meat, California vegetable kabobs notwithstanding. Yet this charmer, one of the best new restaurants in the East Bay, has such extraordinary vegetables that word began to spread among local vegetarians soon after it opened. You'll find zucchini cakes with scallions, paprika, and garlicky yogurt for dipping; borek with spinach and feta; incredible Turkish fries seasoned with spices from Turkey; and a sublime bulgur pilaf. There is always a seasonal vegetable pilaf and the salads are utterly flawless. As long as the aroma of grilled meat does not offend your vegetarian sensibilities, Ephesus is one of the best destinations in the East Bay for an outstanding vegetarian meal.

VEGETARIAN FRIENDLY

★★/$$
4. Julia's Kitchen at COPIA

500 First Street (at Soscal Avenue)
Napa, CA
707.265.5700

CALIFORNIA-FRENCH

Hours:	Mon-Wed 11:30 a.m. to 3:00 p.m.
	Th-Sun 5:30 p.m. to 9:30 p.m.
Payment:	Credit cards
Parking:	Large free lot
Atmosphere:	Elegant

COPIA is the imposing center for food and the arts in downtown Napa. With its art installations, galleries, museums, edible landscaping, and diverse programs, it is considered a Mecca for foodies. Julia's Kitchen is COPIA's main dining room. Much of the produce served here is from the center's gardens, which are overseen by Jeff Dawson (who counts among his credits time spent as Apple Computer CEO Steve Jobs's personal gardener). Among the selections vegetarians might find tempting are roasted beet salad with a vinaigrette made with Vinaigre de Banyuls, one of the finest vinegars in the world; baby carrot salad with leeks and curry dressing; and ravioli with Italian beans, broccoli rabe, and preserved lemons. There are not a lot of vegan selections. Other dining options at COPIA include the American Market Cafe and the Wine Spectator Tasting Table. All are operated by The Patina Group, a corporate food-service operation based in Los Angeles.

VEGETARIAN FRIENDLY

★★/$
5. Latino's Pupuseria & Restaurante El Salvador

1220 Monterey Street (at Tennessee Street)
Vallejo, CA
707.645.9827

SALVADORAN

Hours:	Daily 9:00 a.m. to 6:00 p.m.
Payment:	Cash
Parking:	Easy street parking
Atmosphere:	Very casual

Pupuserias are common throughout the East Bay and this little hole-in-the-wall is one of the best. Pupusas are disks of fried masa stuffed with various ingredients, including zucchini, cheese, and jalapeños, and served with curtido (pickled cabbage) alongside. Black beans, fried plantain, and steamed yucca are also delicious. If you're driving north on highway 80, this delicious little place is about five minutes from the freeway and far superior to the fast-food restaurants at nearly every exit.

VEGETARIAN FRIENDLY

★★/$
6. Small World

932 Coombs Street (near First Street)
Napa, CA
707.224.7743

MIDDLE EASTERN

Hours:	Mon-Fri 8:00 a.m. to 6:00 p.m.
	Sat 9:00 a.m. to 4:00 p.m.
	Closed Sun
Payment:	Credit cards
Parking:	Easy street parking
Atmosphere:	Very casual

For casual down-to-earth fare without the pretensions of some of the valley's tonier eateries, check out Small World. You'll find excellent smoothies made with frozen yogurt, vegetarian pitas (we like the grilled zucchini), veggie tacos with hummus, vegetarian omelettes (served until 11:30 a.m.), and great salad platters.

VEGETARIAN FRIENDLY

★★/$
7. Vegevillage

18350 Sonoma Highway (at Vallejo Avenue)
Boyes Hot Springs, CA
707.939.8383

TAIWANESE

Hours:	Tue-Sat 11:00 a.m. to 8:30 p.m.
	Sun 4:00 p.m. to 8:30 p.m.
	Closed Mon
Payment:	Credit cards (no AmEx)
Parking:	Moderately difficult street parking
Atmosphere:	Casual, mid-scale

The food here reveals the heritage and vegetarian background of its young owners, who are from Taiwan. A menu that features photographs of all the selections presents an eerie picture of faux meats of every sort, images that can be distressing to vegetarians who want their food to look like vegetables rather than the animal foods they are avoiding. But rest assured, there is no real meat, chicken, or seafood in anything. As is often the case, it is the true vegetable dishes that soar with lively flavor here. A broth of seaweed and tomato with little jewels of tofu sparkles on the palate, asparagus and oranges over lettuce are bright and refreshing, and seaweed rolls are unusual and very good. The mock meat selections are perfect for vegetarians still going through animal-protein withdrawal.

VEGETARIAN

★★★/$$$

8. Wine Spectator Restaurant (at the Culinary Institute of America at Greystone)

2555 Main Street
St. Helena, CA
707.967.1010

CALIFORNIAN

Hours:	Sun–Th 11:30 p.m. to 9:00 p.m.
	Fri–Sat 11:30 p.m. to 10:00 p.m.
Payment:	Credit cards
Parking:	Large free lot
Atmosphere:	Casual, upscale, outside dining

In warm weather, a meal on the terrace of this historic building is a delight. Inside is always a pleasure, too, though you might want to get a corner table if noise bothers you; when full, the restaurant is loud. As is the case with any restaurant that focuses on genuine California cuisine, the Wine Spectator Restaurant features high-quality produce—much of it from the CIA's own gardens—that presents excellent options for vegetarians. Butternut squash soup with toasted pumpkin seed oil; endive salad with roasted Asian pear vinaigrette; wild mushroom risotto; and vegetarian cannelloni with sautéed fall greens, hazelnuts, and fresh sage are among the selections available in the cooler months. In the summer, look for anything with heirloom tomatoes. And while you're here, check out the large store downstairs, the museum, and the course offerings, many of which are suitable for the home cook.

VEGETARIAN FRIENDLY

San Francisco

★★/$$
1. All You Knead

> 1466 Haight Street (near Ashbury)
> San Francisco, CA
> 415.552.4550

AMERICAN

Hours:	Daily 8:00 a.m. to 11:00 p.m.
Payment:	Credit cards
Parking:	Difficult street parking
Atmosphere:	Casual urban diner, lively

Hugely popular for breakfast, All You Knead offers more vegetarian options than most traditional American eateries. Breakfast, served until 5:00 p.m. each day, offers a veggie scramble (with eggs, not tofu); an omelette filled with black beans, salsa, and cheddar cheese; and yummy home fries with olives, onions, cheddar, and salsa. Crepes are good and interesting; vegans will enjoy the one with smoked tofu and vegetables in peanut sauce. There are excellent vegetable sandwiches (we prefer the veggie picante with its green chiles), a good vegetable lasagne, and plenty of salads. Pizzas and calzones can always be made either vegetarian or vegan.

VEGETARIAN FRIENDLY

★★/$$
2. Amira Restaurant

590 Valencia Street (at 17th Street)
San Francisco, CA
415.621.6213

MIDDLE EASTERN

Hours:	Tue-Sun 5:30 p.m. to 11:00 p.m.
	Closed Mon
Payment:	Credit cards
Parking:	Difficult street parking
Atmosphere:	Moody, casually elegant and lively

With lush velvet cushions, brass tabletops, candles, and warm sand-colored walls, the interior of Amira is mesmerizing and luxurious. At night, when either belly dancers or gypsy musicians take over, it becomes even more so. You'll quickly sink into a dreamy fog, enhanced by the flavorful foods inspired primarily by Turkey, Lebanon, Libya, Morocco, and Greece. Given the importance of meat in these cultures, it is surprising how many excellent vegetarian choices there are here. For entrées, you'll find vegetable Kushari with bulgur wheat, lentils, and vegetables topped with nuts and sautéed onions with either yogurt salad or tahini sauce alongside. There are two vegan plates and outstanding appetizers and salads that anyone can enjoy.

VEGETARIAN FRIENDLY

★★★/$
3. Ananda Fuara

1298 Market Street (near 9th Street)
San Francisco, CA
415.621.1994

INTERNATIONAL

Hours:	Mon-Tue, Th-Sat 8:00 a.m. to 8:00 p.m.
	Wed 8:00 a.m. to 3:00 p.m.
	Closed Sun
Payment:	Cash, traveler's checks,
	local checks
Parking:	Two public lots within a block
Atmosphere:	Casual urban diner

This hugely popular downtown location is an oasis of intelligent, delicious vegetarian food. The house specialty, "meatloaf" (brown rice, ricotta, eggs, tofu, onions, and spices), with mashed potatoes and mushroom gravy, has reached near-legendary status among vegetarians. You'll also find vegetarian burritos, veggie burgers, samosas with chutney, and an excellent breakfast menu that includes buttermilk pancakes, omelettes, and scrambled tofu. The traditional lassis are excellent. Ananda Fuara is operated by disciples of Sri Chinmoy, an Indian spiritual leader. Servers are clad in colorful saris, and an overhead television shows Sri Chinmoy completing his daily exercises and playing a variety of musical instruments.

VEGETARIAN

★★/$
4. Angkor Borei

3471 Mission Street
  (between Cortland and Kingston)
San Francisco, CA
415.550.8417

CAMBODIAN

Hours:	Mon-Sat 11:00 a.m. to 10:30 p.m.
	Sun 2:00 p.m. to 10:30 p.m.
Payment:	Credit cards
Parking:	Moderately difficult street parking
Atmosphere:	Casual, beautiful

A crepe filled with shredded coconut, tofu, and bean sprouts with a lemon-garlic dipping sauce; vegetarian clay pot "duck"; rock-bottom prices; and generous hospitality are what keep vegetarians coming back to this invitingly homey establishment. The menu is heavy on meat and seafood but the flavors of the vegetarian dishes are so pure and focused and the staff so helpful to vegetarian needs that we believe it is an excellent choice when you find yourself in the Outer Mission.

VEGETARIAN FRIENDLY

★★/$
5. Bok Choy Gardens

> 1820 Clement Street (near 19th Avenue)
> San Francisco, CA
> 415.387.8111

CHINESE

Hours:	Sun, Tue-Th 11:00 a.m. to 9:00 p.m.
	Fri-Sat 11:00 a.m. to 9:30 p.m.
	Closed Mon
Payment:	Credit cards (no AmEx)
Parking:	Medium to difficult street parking
Atmosphere:	Casual urban diner

Vegans can enjoy almost everything offered here, and the take-out service and full catering are at least as popular as the dining room offerings. Quality is consistent throughout the menu but we particularly enjoyed shredded black and enoki mushroom and vermicelli soup, sweet corn soup, and pan noodles with shredded vegetables. Salt-and-pepper spicy tofu is one of the better tofu dishes we've had. Lemonade is made fresh from real lemons.

VEGETARIAN

★★/$
6. Crepevine

216 Church Street (at Market)
San Francisco, CA
415.431.4646

MIDDLE EASTERN CREPERY

Hours:	Sun-Th 7:30 a.m. to 11:00 p.m.
	Fri-Sat 7:30 a.m. to midnight
Payment:	Cash and local checks only
Parking:	Easy street parking, free lot
Atmosphere:	Casual, lively

This place is often mistakenly identified as a vegetarian restaurant, but it isn't. You'll find poultry, beef, pork, and seafood among the selections. There are, however, plenty of choices for both vegans and vegetarians. In addition to fairly standard California-Mediterranean sandwiches, salads, and pastas, there are about a dozen egg dishes, a tofu scramble with mushrooms and spinach, and a lot of crepes. For crepes, we like Le Delice (cheddar cheese with glazed onions) and Greek (spinach, olives, almonds, onions, and feta cheese with cucumber yogurt sauce). Sweet crepes include one with Nutella and bananas. You can, if you prefer, create your own combinations. Anyone for Nutella and tofu?

VEGETARIAN FRIENDLY

★★/$
7. Crepevine

> 624 Irving Street (near 7th Avenue)
> San Francisco, CA
> 415.681.5858

MIDDLE EASTERN CREPERY

Hours:	*Sun-Th 7:30 a.m. to 11:00 p.m.*
	Fri-Sat 7:30 a.m. to midnight
Payment:	*Cash and local checks only*
Parking:	*Easy street parking, free lot*
Atmosphere:	*Casual, lively*

See previous page for details.

VEGETARIAN FRIENDLY

★★/$
8. Einstein's Cafe

1336 9th Avenue (between Irving and Judah)
San Francisco, CA
415.665.4840

CALIFORNIAN

Hours:	Daily 11:00 a.m. to 9:00 p.m.
Payment:	Cash, credit cards
Parking:	Moderate street parking
Atmosphere:	Casual, eclectic

Take your social conscience to dine at Einstein's, which serves as an on-the-job training center for inner-city at-risk youth, operated by Golden Gate Community, a nonprofit agency. Soups are made daily; sandwich options include hummus, eggplant, and mixed vegetables. Salads are big and beautiful, and the fresh strawberry lemonade is yummy and refreshing. Because the business is operated by the students, it is a mix of high energy and occasional rude attitude—no surprise when you remind yourself that these are teenagers and that they're learning to channel their energy (and their anger) productively. The chalkboard, with its carefully written equations, is worthy of a special visit.

VEGETARIAN FRIENDLY

★★★★/$$$
9. Fleur de Lys

777 Sutter Street (near Taylor)
San Francisco, CA
415.673.7779

FRENCH

Hours:	*Mon-Th 6:00 p.m. to 9:00 p.m.*
	Fri-Sat 5:30 p.m. to 9:30 p.m.
	Closed Sun
Payment:	*Credit cards*
Parking:	*Valet $12, difficult street parking*
Atmosphere:	*Elegant, upscale*

Fleur de Lys is one of the top restaurants in San Francisco, and one of the prettiest. It is both lively and sophisticated, with top-notch service and prix-fixe menus that offer three, four, or five courses for omnivores, vegetarians, or vegans. Chef Hubert Keller, an unpretentious, friendly, gracious, and extremely talented Frenchman, is at the top of his game with creative cuisine that always makes sense and always dazzles. It's a great choice for a special occasion.

VEGETARIAN FRIENDLY

★★/$
10. Golden Era Vegetarian Restaurant

572 O'Farrell Street (near Jones Street)
San Francisco, CA
415.673.3136

VIETNAMESE

Hours:	*Mon, Wed-Sun 11:00 a.m. to 9:00 p.m.*
	Closed Tue
Payment:	*Credit cards (no AmEx)*
Parking:	*Often difficult street parking*
Atmosphere:	*Mid-scale, elegant*

If you notice similarities between Golden Era and Oakland's Golden Lotus, it is no surprise. It is operated by the daughter of the Oakland eatery's owner and its menu is similar. Everything is vegetarian, there are no eggs and no MSG, and much of the food has a bright, lively quality. You'll find a lot of faux meats here, from fish cakes to beef, and they are often identified by carnivorous names like spicy beef stew, ginger fish, and teriyaki chicken. But don't worry, it's all soy or wheat. Try the vegetarian lamb clay pot or the wonton noodle soup. When it comes to beverages, salted plum lemonade and carrot juice are wonderful.

VEGETARIAN

★★★★/$$$
11. Greens

Fort Mason Center Building A (near Buchanan)
San Francisco, CA
415.771.6222

CALIFORNIAN

Hours:	Mon 5:30 p.m. to 9:15 p.m.
	Tue-Fri noon to 2:30 p.m.,
	5:30 p.m. to 9:15 p.m.
	Sat noon to 2:30 p.m.,
	5:30 p.m. to 9:00 p.m.
	Sun 10:00 a.m. to 2:00 p.m.
Payment:	Credit cards
Parking:	Free lot
Atmosphere:	Light, airy, relaxed, upscale

Greens was the first Bay Area restaurant to elevate vegetarian cuisine to the level of fine dining, and its first chef—acclaimed cookbook author Deborah Madison—set the bar high for all who follow in her footsteps. Annie Sommerville has headed the kitchen for years now, maintaining a steady, if not particularly innovative, course. Greens is what it has always been and that's no small feat. The menu changes daily, there is a strong commitment to local organic produce, and preparations are nearly always flawless. Vegans will need to inquire about cheese and butter, but vegetarians can browse and choose with abandon. Greens' black bean soup is legendary. One of our favorite menu items is a corn and grilled-onion tart with local St. George cheese and sage, with grilled zucchini tossed in poblano butter and sautéed greens with pumpkin seeds alongside. As good as the food is, the view is even better. Greens sits on the edge of the San Francisco Bay and offers a window onto boats, seals, ships heading in and out of the gate, and the glorious bridge, which at certain times glows in the afternoon sun.

VEGETARIAN

★★/$
12. Haveli

35 Sixth Street (at Market)
San Francisco, CA
415.348.1381

INDIAN

Hours:	Daily 10:00 a.m. to 4:00 p.m.
Payment:	Credit cards (no AmEx)
Parking:	Difficult street parking, parking garage nearby
Atmosphere:	Quiet, casual

This almost-vegan restaurant (there's yogurt and a bit of cheese) defines its cuisine as Hindu. Inside, a spare, calm interior provides a refreshing respite to the urban grit of Sixth Street, one of the tougher neighborhoods in the city. Most of the fare here is typically Indian, with curried potatoes, curried vegetables, vegetable-filled samosas, and kachori (round pastries filled with spicy lentils).

VEGETARIAN WITH MANY VEGAN OPTIONS

★★/$$

13. Herbivore

983 Valencia Street (near 21st Street)
San Francisco, CA
415.826.5657

INTERNATIONAL

Hours:	Sun-Th 11:00 a.m. to 10:00 p.m.
	Fri-Sat 11:00 a.m. to 11:00 p.m.
Payment:	Credit cards (no AmEx)
Parking:	Moderately difficult street parking,
	public lot around the corner
Atmosphere:	Mid-scale, casual, trendy, quiet

Vegetarians with big appetites flock to this
Mission District eatery. The best selections are
those that showcase the restaurant's commit-
ment to excellent produce, such as a vegetable
sampler, green papaya salad, curry-coconut udon
noodles, the dazzling lemongrass noodles, and
silver noodle salad. New vegetarians can satisfy
their meat cravings with charbroiled seitan, and
vegans can rest assured that there are no dairy
products lurking anywhere. A good beer-and-
wine list and intriguing desserts round out the
appealing menu.

VEGAN

★★/$$
14. Herbivore

531 Divisidero Street (at Fell Street)
San Francisco, CA
415.885.7133

INTERNATIONAL

Hours:	Sun-Th 11:00 a.m. to 10:00 p.m.
	Fri-Sat 11:00 a.m. to 11:00 p.m.
Payment:	Credit cards (no AmEx)
Parking:	Medium difficult street parking
Atmosphere:	Mid-scale, casual

See previous page for details. In addition, this location serves brunch on weekends, one of the only fully vegan brunch options around.

VEGAN

★★★/$

15. Hulu House

754 Kirkham (near 12th Avenue)
San Francisco, CA
415.682.0826

SINGAPOREAN

Hours:	Mon, Wed-Sun 11:00 a.m. to 9:00 p.m. Closed Tue
Payment:	Credit cards (no AmEx)
Parking:	Fairly easy street parking
Atmosphere:	Casual, peaceful, clean, friendly

Hulu House is hugely popular with the Asian vegetarian community, always a good sign. Not only are there no animal products here, there is no garlic and no onion either. Still, the cuisine is bright and fresh. Hulu House is run by Buddhist vegetarians and it is said that they began with all new equipment that had never been touched by animal products. Although they rely on many mock meats, the cooks manage to create traditional dishes that have an amazing degree of authentic taste. Malaysian laksa (hard to find even in nonvegetarian restaurants), Singapore noodles, pickled vegetables with chiles, coconut rice with faux fish, plump rice noodles with vegetables, fresh light spring rolls, and outstanding teas are among the superb dishes that keep regulars coming back again and again.

VEGETARIAN

★★/$
16. Jay's Cheesesteak

553 Divisidero Street (between Fell and Hayes)
San Francisco, CA
415.771.5104

AMERICAN

Hours:	*Daily 11:00 a.m. to 10:00 p.m.*
Payment:	*Cash only*
Parking:	*Difficult street parking,*
	paid lot next door
Atmosphere:	*Very casual fast food*

You'd never suspect that a cheesesteak joint would be so vegan-friendly, but that's exactly what this place is, with nearly a dozen seitan sandwiches on the menu and a sign explaining what, exactly, seitan is. Although Jay's is known for its excellent Philly-style steak sandwiches, the vegetarian versions are clearly more than gratuitous.

VEGETARIAN FRIENDLY

★★/$
17. Jay's Cheesesteak

3285 21st Street (at Valencia)
San Francisco, CA
415.285.5200

AMERICAN

Hours:	*Daily 11:00 a.m. to 10:00 p.m.*
Payment:	*Cash only*
Parking:	*Moderate street parking*
Atmosphere:	*Very casual fast food*

See previous page for details.

VEGETARIAN FRIENDLY

★★★/$
18. Juicy Lucy's

703 Columbus Avenue (at Filbert)
San Francisco, CA
415.786.1285

JUICE BAR

Hours:	Change seasonally, call ahead
Payment:	Cash only
Parking:	Very difficult street parking
Atmosphere:	Juice bar, lively, urban, alternative

The delicious juices here—several dozen kinds—are 100 percent organic, as is virtually everything served in this little place, from baked tofu sandwiches and lovely soups to bright seasonal salads. Nearly everything is raw as well, and satisfies the requirements not only of vegan diets but also of macrobiotics. Juicy Lucy's has been mentioned in *Gourmet Magazine*, so you have to figure they're doing something right.

VEGETARIAN

★★/$
19. Kan Zaman

1793 Haight Street (at Shrader Street)
San Francisco, CA
415.751.9656

MIDDLE EASTERN

Hours:	Mon-Fri 5:00 p.m. to midnight
	Sat-Sun noon to midnight
	Fri-Sat noon to 2 p.m. for cocktails
Payment:	Credit cards (no AmEx)
Parking:	Difficult street parking
Atmosphere:	Lively, colorful, festive

At Kan Zaman, the hummus tingles with lemon
and the baba ganoush is smoky, but other dishes,
such as tired favas with garlic and soggy
spinach pie, can be disappointing. Still, belly
dancing, hot mulled wine, and a party atmosphere make this a fun destination. It's a great
place for large groups.

VEGETARIAN FRIENDLY

★★/$
20. Lucky Creation

854 Washington Street (near Grant)
San Francisco, CA
415.989.0818

CHINESE

Hours:	Mon-Tue, Th-Sun 11:00 a.m. to 9:30 p.m.
	Closed Wed
Payment:	Cash, traveler's checks, local checks
Parking:	Difficult street parking, public lot a block away
Atmosphere:	Casual urban diner

Lucky Creation is the only 100 percent vegetarian restaurant that remains in Chinatown, which is rather shocking given the growing number of vegetarians in San Francisco, including in this part of the city. Here you'll find a fairly standard mix of vegetables and faux meats, with an emphasis on traditional Chinese preparations. Sweet corn and white mushroom soup, straw mushrooms with corn and rice soup, cabbage and noodle soup, and generous rice plates are bone-warming and soul-satisfying. Spring rolls are light and delicate and even the pot stickers are yummy. Lucky Creation Bean Thread Soup is also quite good.

VEGETARIAN

★★/$
21. Mandalay Restaurant

4348 California (at Sixth Avenue)
San Francisco, CA
415.386.3896

Burmese

Hours:	*Daily 11:30 a.m. to 9:30 p.m.*
Payment:	*Credit cards*
Parking:	*Easy street parking*
Atmosphere:	*Quiet, mid-scale*

The shockingly inexpensive fare here is not vegetarian, but a fresh ginger salad is reason enough to bring anyone in, including a number of neighborhood regulars who arrive daily to enjoy it for lunch. The green beans are outstanding, too, and the menu offers several other vegetarian choices. But get the ginger salad.

Vegetarian friendly

★★★★/$$$
22. Millennium

580 Geary (near Jones)
San Francisco, CA
415.345.3900

INTERNATIONAL

Hours:	Sun-Th 5:30 p.m. to 9:30 p.m.
	Fri-Sat 5:30 p.m. to 10:00 p.m.
Payment:	Credit cards
Parking:	Free street parking after 6:00 p.m., public garage nearby
Atmosphere:	Elegant, upscale

Millennium elevates vegan cooking to a new elegance in a formal dining room at the Savoy Hotel. Chef Eric Tucker takes his inspiration from cuisines all over the world and employs excellent organic products to express his vision. Salads are layered with flavors that combine strawberries with sherry vinegar, sage oil with fennel pollen, and smoky tofu with sweet and tangy balsamic vinegar. Entrées offer several raw plates; earthy stews like braised French lentils with grilled polenta and chanterelles; and a vegetarian version of the Brazilian national dish, feijoada, with black beans and spicy habañero cream. The menu changes frequently, as it must to follow the seasons. Although there have been missteps and periods when quality has dipped, in early 2004 Millennium was as good as it had ever been.

VEGAN

★★/$$
23. Miss Millie's

4123 24th Street (near Diamond)
San Francisco, CA
415.285.5598

AMERICAN

Hours:	Wed-Sat 6:00 p.m. to 10:00 p.m.
	Closed Mon-Tue
Payment:	Credit cards (no AmEx)
Parking:	Difficult street parking, public lot
	two blocks away
Atmosphere:	Lively, retro elegance

The Bay Area is a jaded market when it comes to restaurants. There is such a wealth of ingredients and talent that it can be hard to get locals excited. Yet Miss Millie's does just that—with a quirky exuberance and inventive but sensible dishes that reference but do not duplicate traditional American foods. Warm farro with roasted butternut squash, raisins, crème fraiche, and toasted pecans is positively addictive, and grits with white cheddar cheese is warming and satisfying. A crepe filled with locally produced fresh ricotto and candied Meyer lemon is to die for, and roasted potatoes with spinach, garlic, onions, and cheddar cheese are about as good as spuds get. Entrées include an excellent white bean cassoulet, yummy macaroni and cheese, and wild mushroom enchiladas. Only about a quarter of the menu is vegetarian but the quality is top-notch. Decor is eccentric, chic, and homey, like an upscale dive or fancy hole-in-the-wall.

VEGETARIAN FRIENDLY

★★/$
24. New Ganges Restaurant

775 Frederick Street (near Stanyan)
San Francisco, CA
415.681.4355

INDIAN

Hours:	*Daily 11:00 a.m. to 2:00 p.m.,*
	5:00 p.m. to 10:00 p.m.
Payment:	*Credit cards (no AmEx)*
Parking:	*Moderate street parking*
Atmosphere:	*Casual, homey*

For more than two decades, The Ganges offered extraordinary vegetarian cuisine prepared by Malvi Doshi, a gracious matriarch whose husband worked at her side. After his death, Malvi sold her restaurant and wrote *Cooking Along the Ganges* (iUniverse, 2002), a follow-up to *A Surti Touch* (Strawberry Hill, 1980). Now we have the New Ganges, which offers good, fresh Indian fare in a fairly harsh atmosphere without the luxurious cushions and carpets and soft lighting of the original. Still, the food is good and true. Cauliflower pakora, potato-spinach pakora, and channa masala (chickpea curry) are deservedly popular, and saag paneer is among the best versions around. Don't forget to order raita. Fans of the original Ganges will be happy to know that there is a version of the famous banana curry, though here the fruit is mashed and mixed with coconut, cilantro, lemon, and spices rather than stuffed with the mixture.

VEGETARIAN

★★★/$$
25. Piperade

1015 Battery Street (at Green)
San Francisco, CA
415.391.2555

CONTEMPORARY BASQUE

Hours:	Mon-Fri 11:30 a.m. to 3:00 p.m., 5:30 p.m. to 11:00 p.m.
	Sat 5:30 p.m. to 11:00 p.m.
	Closed Sun
Payment:	Credit cards
Parking:	Moderately difficult street parking
Atmosphere:	Casual, mid-scale

Previously known as Pastis, Piperade is perhaps the most personal restaurant yet from Chef Gerald Hirogoyen, long ranked among the top chefs in the United States. The focus on Basque cuisine returns Hirogoyen to his roots, and there may be no better Basque restaurant in the country today, certainly not in the city. Although there is abundant meat and seafood on the menu, the quality of produce and the command of techniques in the vegetarian dishes make this an excellent choice, especially when those of disparate diets dine together. Among the vegetarian selections are cornmeal flat bread with goat cheese, leeks, and caramelized onions; and an addictive white bean salad with eggs and chives (ask to hold the anchovies); and an ethereal asparagus flan and warm peppers with goat cheese, raisins, and moscotel vinaigrette. Given the level of quality at Piperade, prices are quite reasonable.

VEGETARIAN FRIENDLY

★★★/$
26. Piperade Cafe

Icehouse Alley
*   (between Union & Green and Sansome & Battery)*
San Francisco, CA
415.402.4892

CAFE

Hours:	Mon-Fri, 7:30 a.m. to 3:00 p.m.
	Closed Sat-Sun
Payment:	Credit cards
Parking:	Moderate street parking
Atmosphere:	Fast food takeout

This little sister cafe of Piperade is charming and sweet, as little sisters often are. Given the charm of owners Gerald and Cameron Hirogoyen, it would be a surprise if it weren't. There are good teas and excellent coffee drinks, sensible rather than silly, and reasonably priced. If you're looking for an alternative to a Starbucks latte, you'll find it here. You'll also find excellent breakfast items (French pastries, bagels, oatmeal, yogurt, fruit), soups, salads, sandwiches, vegetarian quiche, and good sparkling drinks like limonata and aranciata.

VEGETARIAN FRIENDLY

★★★/$$
27. Q

225 Clement Street (near 3rd Avenue)
San Francisco, CA
415.752.2298

AMERICAN

Hours:	*Mon-Sat 11:00 a.m. to 11:00 p.m.*
	Sun 11:00 a.m. to 10:00 p.m.
Payment:	*Credit cards (no AmEx)*
Parking:	*Difficult street parking*
Atmosphere:	*Lively, urban, casual*

In a perfect world, a lot of restaurants would look like Q, with its homey comfort, emphasis on quality ingredients, and excellent techniques. The egalitarian menu offers vegetarian and meat entrées side by side, neither deemed more important than the other. This restaurant is clearly a labor of love rather than an architect-and-consultant-driven enterprise; as such, it is utterly refreshing and charming. Vegetarian selections are printed in green, a subtle and elegant way to indicate them. You'll find robust preparations like grilled corn on the cob with spicy lime butter, a platter of grilled vegetables, and potato fritters with smoky tomato salsa. Also offered are outstanding sides like spicy coleslaw, braised vegetables, black beans, and garlicky spinach. Entrées include grilled squash, corn, sweet potatoes, mushrooms, carrots and onions served with black beans, wild rice pilaf, and delicious marinated beets. There's mushroom risotto with spinach as well as macaroni and cheese. Although the meat entrées will put off strict vegans, Q is an excellent place for committed carnivores and die-hard vegetarians to enjoy a lusty meal together.

VEGETARIAN FRIENDLY

★★/$
28. Reggae Runnins Village Store and Restaurant

505 Divisidero (near Fell)
San Francisco, CA
415.922.2442

JAMAICAN

Hours:	Mon-Sat 11:00 a.m. to 7:00 p.m.
	Sun noon to 5:00 p.m.
Payment:	Credit cards (no AmEx)
Parking:	Moderate street parking
Atmosphere:	Rustic, in-store cafe

Reggae Runnins Village Store and Restaurant is the only place in the Bay Area to find vegan versions of jerked chicken and other island specialties (such as Jamaican beans and rice) and also have your dreadlocks professionally maintained. The menu changes daily; among the selections are stir-fried plantain, plantain stew, jerked tofu burgers with house-made jerk sauce, and Rundown Stew with peas and rice. Be sure to try the Rasta Pasta. The store includes a selection of traditional ethnic clothing, hats, and crafts.

MOSTLY VEGAN

★★★★/$$
29. Samovar Tea Lounge

498 Sanchez Street (at 18th Street)
San Francisco, CA
415.626.4700

INTERNATIONAL

Hours:	Daily 9:00 a.m. to 10:00 p.m.
Payment:	Credit cards (no AmEx)
Parking:	Moderately difficult street parking
Atmosphere:	Trendy, urban, friendly

Samovar Tea Lounge has broadened the service of tea beyond the previous options of English-style afternoon tea or Japanese-style tea. With carefully selected teas from around the world, Samovar offers an extraordinary experience to the novice tea drinker and intriguing choices for tea aficionados. Particularly interesting are the pu-erh teas, some of which are so full-bodied and rich (yet seductively smooth, as well) that they can easily replace coffee. You'll also find excellent white teas. The menu here is equally seductive and although it is not vegetarian, there are excellent selections for both vegetarians and vegans. Look for noodle soup in green tea broth with minced vegetables and seaweed, tofu baked with ginger served over oolong rice with toasted nori and homemade pickles, seared vegetarian pot stickers, and grilled tofu sandwiches. For dessert, don't miss the bergamot bread pudding (not for vegans), tea-infused shortbread, and chai spice cake.

VEGETARIAN FRIENDLY

★★/$
30. The San Francisco Soup Company

201 Mission Street (near Beale Street)
San Francisco, CA
415.278.9878

Soup

Hours:	Mon-Fri 7:00 a.m. to 4:00 p.m. Closed Sat-Sun
Payment:	Credit cards
Parking:	Difficult street parking, public lot nearby
Atmosphere:	Very casual

The San Francisco Soup Company is quickly becoming a city institution, widely praised for its freshly made soups, available in pleasant dining rooms with ample counter space or as takeout, the most popular part of the endeavor. Nearly a dozen soups are available each day, chosen from scores that are rotated throughout the year. You'll always find a couple of vegan soups, along with five or six that are completely vegetarian. Among the selections are Creole Vegetable, Smoky Split Pea, Gazpacho, Cauliflower Ginger, Chilled Cucumber and Avocado, Garden Vegetable Chowder, Indian Lentil, Portobello and Barley, Red Bell Pepper and Lime, Szechuan Carrot, Tomato Fennel, Vegetarian Tortilla, and Zucchini and Blue Cheese.

VEGETARIAN FRIENDLY

★★/$
31. The San Francisco Soup Company

One Market Street (Bayside Food Court)
San Francisco, CA
415.495.4765

SOUP

Hours:	Mon-Fri 7:00 a.m. to 4:00 p.m.
	Closed Sat-Sun
Payment:	Credit cards
Parking:	Difficult street parking, public lot nearby
Atmosphere:	Very casual

The San Francisco Soup Company is quickly becoming a city institution, widely praised for its freshly made soups, available in pleasant dining rooms with ample counter space or as takeout, the most popular part of the endeavor. Nearly a dozen soups are available each day, chosen from scores that are rotated throughout the year. You'll always find a couple of vegan soups, along with five or six that are completely vegetarian. Among the selections are Creole Vegetable, Smoky Split Pea, Gazpacho, Cauliflower Ginger, Chilled Cucumber and Avocado, Garden Vegetable Chowder, Indian Lentil, Portobello and Barley, Red Bell Pepper and Lime, Szechuan Carrot, Tomato Fennel, Vegetarian Tortilla, and Zucchini and Blue Cheese.

VEGETARIAN FRIENDLY

★★★/$

32. The San Francisco Soup Company

50 Post Street (at the Crocker Galleria)
San Francisco, CA
415.397.7188

SOUP

Hours:	Mon-Fri 7:00 a.m. to 5:00 p.m.
	Sat 11:30 a.m. to 4:00 p.m.
	Closed Sun
Payment:	Credit cards
Parking:	Difficult street parking, public lot one block away
Atmosphere:	Very casual

The San Francisco Soup Company is quickly becoming a city institution, widely praised for its freshly made soups, available in pleasant dining rooms with ample counter space or as takeout, the most popular part of the endeavor. Nearly a dozen soups are available each day, chosen from scores that are rotated throughout the year. You'll always find a couple of vegan soups, along with five or six that are completely vegetarian. Among the selections are Creole Vegetable, Smoky Split Pea, Gazpacho, Cauliflower Ginger, Chilled Cucumber and Avocado, Garden Vegetable Chowder, Indian Lentil, Portobello and Barley, Red Bell Pepper and Lime, Szechuan Carrot, Tomato Fennel, Vegetarian Tortilla, and Zucchini and Blue Cheese.

VEGETARIAN FRIENDLY

★★/$

33. The San Francisco Soup Company

221 Montgomery Street (near Bush)
San Francisco, CA
415.834.0472

SOUP

Hours:	Mon-Fri 7:00 a.m. to 4:00 p.m.
	Closed Sat-Sun
Payment:	Credit cards
Parking:	Difficult street parking, public lot nearby
Atmosphere:	Very casual

The San Francisco Soup Company is quickly becoming a city institution, widely praised for its freshly made soups, available in pleasant dining rooms with ample counter space or as takeout, the most popular part of the endeavor. Nearly a dozen soups are available each day, chosen from scores that are rotated throughout the year. You'll always find a couple of vegan soups, along with five or six that are completely vegetarian. Among the selections are Creole Vegetable, Smoky Split Pea, Gazpacho, Cauliflower Ginger, Chilled Cucumber and Avocado, Garden Vegetable Chowder, Indian Lentil, Portobello and Barley, Red Bell Pepper and Lime, Szechuan Carrot, Tomato Fennel, Vegetarian Tortilla, and Zucchini and Blue Cheese.

VEGETARIAN FRIENDLY

★★/$

34. The San Francisco Soup Company

142 2nd Street (near Mission)
San Francisco, CA
415.593.7687

SOUP

Hours:	Mon-Fri 7:00 a.m. to 4:00 p.m.
	Closed Sat-Sun
Payment:	Credit cards
Parking:	Difficult street parking, public lot nearby
Atmosphere:	Very casual

The San Francisco Soup Company is quickly becoming a city institution, widely praised for its freshly made soups, available in pleasant dining rooms with ample counter space or as takeout, the most popular part of the endeavor. Nearly a dozen soups are available each day, chosen from scores that are rotated throughout the year. You'll always find a couple of vegan soups, along with five or six that are completely vegetarian. Among the selections are Creole Vegetable, Smoky Split Pea, Gazpacho, Cauliflower Ginger, Chilled Cucumber and Avocado, Garden Vegetable Chowder, Indian Lentil, Portobello and Barley, Red Bell Pepper and Lime, Szechuan Carrot, Tomato Fennel, Vegetarian Tortilla, and Zucchini and Blue Cheese.

VEGETARIAN FRIENDLY

★★/$
35. The San Francisco Soup Company

531 Diamond (near Battery Avenue)
San Francisco, CA
415.788.7687

Soup

Hours:	Mon-Fri 7:00 a.m. to 4:00 p.m.
	Closed Sat-Sun
Payment:	Credit cards
Parking:	Difficult street parking, public lot nearby
Atmosphere:	Very casual

The San Francisco Soup Company is quickly becoming a city institution, widely praised for its freshly made soups, available in pleasant dining rooms with ample counter space or as takeout, the most popular part of the endeavor. Nearly a dozen soups are available each day, chosen from scores that are rotated throughout the year. You'll always find a couple of vegan soups, along with five or six that are completely vegetarian. Among the selections are Creole Vegetable, Smoky Split Pea, Gazpacho, Cauliflower Ginger, Chilled Cucumber and Avocado, Garden Vegetable Chowder, Indian Lentil, Portobello and Barley, Red Bell Pepper and Lime, Szechuan Carrot, Tomato Fennel, Vegetarian Tortilla, and Zucchini and Blue Cheese.

VEGETARIAN FRIENDLY

★★/$
36. Shangri-La

2026 Irving Street (near 21st Avenue)
San Francisco, CA
415.731.2548

CHINESE

Hours:	Daily 11:30 a.m. to 9:00 p.m.
	Closed 1st & 3rd Wed of
	each month
Payment:	Credit cards (no AmEx)
Parking:	Difficult street parking
Atmosphere:	Casual urban diner

The menu here is riddled with mistakes in grammar and vocabulary, making it an interesting and amusing read. But you have to wonder about some of the names: Vegetal goose? Vegetal kidney? Shark Fin Vegetable Plate? If you want to pretend you're eating meat, this is the place for you. We like lotus fruit with carrots and snow peas, golden corn and mushroom soup, Mongolian black moss soup, and the pot stickers. Mu shu pancakes with sliced vegetables, eggplant with basil, and mustard greens with bean curd sheets are both interesting and tasty.

VEGETARIAN

★★/$

37. Soups

784 O'Farrell Street (near Larkin Street)
San Francisco, CA
415.775.6406

Soup

Hours:	Daily 10:00 a.m. to 6:30 p.m.
Payment:	Cash, traveler's checks, local checks
Parking:	Difficult street parking
Atmosphere:	Very casual

If any neighborhood in San Francisco deserves a good soup joint, it's the Tenderloin, long considered one of the city's diciest areas. Thanks to owner Richard Gaule, Soups is it. Gaule has been serving up outstanding soups for more than ten years. These days, there are about six soups available at any given time, along with hot dogs, veggie hot dogs, and a few simple sandwiches. There are always vegetarian soups such as hearty vegetable and potato. The price (around $4) includes a half-bowl refill, a drink, and crackers.

VEGETARIAN FRIENDLY

★★/$
38. Sunrise Deli

2115 Irving (near 23rd Avenue)
San Francisco, CA
415.664.8210

LEBANESE

Hours:	Mon-Sat 9:00 a.m. to 6:00 p.m.
	Sun 9:00 a.m. to 5:00 p.m.
Payment:	Credit cards (no AmEx)
Parking:	Easy street parking
Atmosphere:	Very casual

The generous vegan veggie plate is reason enough to visit this pleasant Middle Eastern deli that, although not exclusively vegetarian, is hugely popular with the local vegetarian community. Excellent hummus, baba ganoush, and other outstanding traditional dishes are also offered here.

VEGETARIAN FRIENDLY WITH VEGAN OPTIONS

★★/$
39. Truly Mediterranean

3109 16th Street (near Valencia)
San Francisco, CA
415.252.7482

MIDDLE EASTERN

Hours:	Mon-Th 11:00 a.m. to 11:00 p.m.
	Fri-Sat 11:00 a.m. to midnight
	Sun 11:00 a.m. to 10:00 p.m.
Payment:	Credit cards (no AmEx)
Parking:	Difficult street parking
Atmosphere:	Very casual

Not much bigger than a closet (and about the size of some New York apartments), Truly Mediterranean is bright and clean, with excellent food that is popular with vegetarians and vegans in spite of the meat offerings. The condiments and salads—hummus, baba ganoush, tabbouleh, cucumber-yogurt—are first-rate, and the falafel is outstanding. Be sure to get the fried potatoes and eggplant alongside. And do not miss the extraordinary yogurt drink spiked with mint and garlic; it is sensational. Mostly takeout.

VEGETARIAN FRIENDLY

★★/$
40. Truly Mediterranean

1724 Haight Street (at Cole)
San Francisco, CA
415.751.7482

MIDDLE EASTERN

Hours:	Mon-Th 11:00 a.m. to 11:00 p.m.
	Fri-Sat 11:00 a.m. to midnight
	Sun 11:00 a.m. to 10:00 p.m.
Payment:	Credit cards (no AmEx)
Parking:	Difficult street parking
Atmosphere:	Very casual

See previous page for details.

VEGETARIAN FRIENDLY

★★/$$
41. 2202 Oxygen Bar

795 Valencia (at 19th Street)
San Francisco, CA
415.255.2102

Raw Vegetarian

Hours:	*Tue & Th 7:00 p.m. to 11:00 p.m.*
Payment:	*Credit cards*
Parking:	*Difficult street parking*
Atmosphere:	*Trendy, hip*

Apparently, one cannot live on oxygen alone. Two nights a week, guest chefs prepare a raw vegetarian meal to serve up alongside this hip bar's standard fare of oxygen and elixirs. The rest of the time you'll have to go elsewhere or get by on air ($20 for a 40-minute treatment; all oxygen treatments include aromatherapy) and one of the special herbal elixirs or tinctures blended to enhance everything from energy, mood, and libido to beauty and brain activity (which should, if it is effective, guarantee that you don't need to come back). A mobile oxygen kiosk is available for parties.

Raw vegetarian

★★/$

42. Urban Forage

254 Fillmore Street (at Laussat Street)
San Francisco, CA
415.255.6701

Raw Vegan

Hours:	Mon-Fri 8:00 a.m. to 9:00 p.m.
	Sat-Sun 10:00 a.m. to 9:00 p.m.
Payment:	Credit cards
Parking:	Difficult street parking
Atmosphere:	Trendy, urban casual

Think of it as Roxanne's for the poor urban hipster. Nearly everything on the menu is raw (brown rice with shredded carrots and peanut sauce is a popular exception), and the flavor combinations are innovative if not always completely successful. Selections include carrots, radishes, kimchee, sprouts, and peanut sauce wrapped in a collard leaf or sauerkraut, lettuce, sprouts, and carrots wrapped in a collard leaf. Try the cauliflower "hummus" or portobello mushroom filled with walnut-fennel puree and topped with spinach and miso-tahini sauce. There are good juices and infused teas, to which you can add a dollop of hemp milk if you like. To eat in cozy comfort, head to the dining room upstairs.

Raw vegan

★★/$
43. Vege House

609 Sixth Avenue (near Clement)
San Francisco, CA
415.668.0609

CHINESE & VIETNAMESE

Hours:	*Daily 8:00 a.m. to 6:00 p.m.*
Payment:	*Cash only*
Parking:	*Difficult street parking*
Atmosphere:	*Small, casual, friendly takeout*

In addition to the casual sit-down restaurant that offers fairly typical Chinese and Vietnamese vegetarian fare (lots of marinated faux meats), this location has a small take-out deli that is very popular with neighborhood vegetarians. Fried tofu is a specialty here and both the tofu and soy milk are house-made.

VEGETARIAN

★★★/$$
44. Vicolo Pizza

> 201 Ivy Alley (between Hayes and Grove,
>   off Franklin Street)
> San Francisco, CA
> 415.863.2382

CONTEMPORARY PIZZERIA

Hours:	Mon-Th 5:00 p.m. to 9:30 p.m.
	Fri-Sat 5:00 p.m. to 11:00 p.m.
	Sun 5:00 p.m. to 8:30 p.m.
Payment:	Credit cards
Parking:	Difficult street parking
Atmosphere:	Casual, urban, bright

Sold by the slice and by the pie, the pizzas here are among the best in the city and offer several selections for vegetarians, including a vegetable pizza, a wild mushroom pizza, and a cheeseless pizza. Salads are good options, too, especially the spinach, black bean, and feta. There's a small selection of wines by the glass and good beers on tap and bottled. The out-of-the-way location in Ivy Alley makes Vicolo's feel like a real find, which it is.

VEGETARIAN FRIENDLY

★★/$
45. Vietnamese Sandwiches

426 Larkin (near Golden Gate Avenue)
San Francisco, CA
415.771.3388

VIETNAMESE

Hours:	Mon-Fri 6:30 a.m. to 6:00 p.m.
	Closed Sat-Sun
Payment:	Cash, traveler's checks,
	local checks
Parking:	Medium difficult street parking
Atmosphere:	Very casual

A sandwich for breakfast? You bet. Banh mi are a breakfast tradition in Vietnam and they are delicious and completely satisfying, yet not too filling. It can be hard, though, to find vegetarian versions. The sandwiches are made on soft rolls and include shredded carrots, shredded radish, onions, cilantro, hot peppers, a zingy dressing, and usually some sort of meat or poultry. Here, you'll find versions using tofu and sautéed greens as well.

VEGETARIAN FRIENDLY

★★/$$

46. Zante Pizza and Indian Cuisine

3489 Mission (at Cortland Avenue)
San Francisco, CA
415.821.3949

INDIAN/PIZZA

Hours:	Daily 11:00 a.m. to 3:00 p.m., 5:00 p.m. to 11:00 p.m.
Payment:	Credit cards
Parking:	Moderately difficult street parking
Atmosphere:	Casual, lively

Given the ubiquity of fusion cooking of every sort—French-Asian, California-Italian, Mexican-Japanese—Indian pizza was probably inevitable. And it's not an entirely ludicrous concept, considering India's indigenous flat breads. But the best offerings here are not the pizzas, which in the end are just too muddled to be truly satisfying (though the best are the ones with Indian toppings). The chef here is heavy-handed with the heat, so if you like your curries hot, this is a great destination. You'll find the usual selections: pakoras, samosas, naan with onion, naan with garlic (naan stuffed with mozzarella is a concept that probably will not catch on), potato-cauliflower curry, spinach with herbs and house-made cheese, garbanzo bean curry, and vegetable curry.

VEGETARIAN FRIENDLY

San Mateo County

★★★/$$
1. Bangkok Bay Thai

825 El Camino Real (near Broadway Street)
Redwood City, CA
650.365.5369

THAI

Hours:	Mon-Th 11:00 a.m. to 3:00 p.m.,
	5:00 p.m. to 9:30 p.m.
	Fri 11:00 a.m. to 3:00 p.m.,
	5:00 p.m. to 10:00 p.m.
	Sat-Sun 5:00 p.m. to 9:00 p.m.
Payment:	Credit cards (no AmEx)
Parking:	Free lot in rear
Atmosphere:	Elegant, mid-scale

Four sisters—Neena, Mimi, Cholada, and Ikun—run this beautiful and charming place. Although there is abundant seafood, meat, and poultry on the extensive menu, there are enough delicious vegetarian dishes to warrant inclusion in this book. Soups—hot-and-sour mushroom and lemon mushroom with coconut milk—are flavorful and satisfying (though we recommend adding a couple of spoonsful of steamed rice to those with coconut milk; it adds a layer of flavor and texture that is deeply appealing). All the vegetable curries are out-standing; sweet-and-sour tofu is good; "drunken" noodles and vegetarian fried rice are excellent. If you ask for things medium spicy or spicy, they're even better.

VEGETARIAN FRIENDLY

★★/$$
2. Bangkok Cuisine

407 Lytton Avenue (near Waverly Street)
Palo Alto, CA
650.322.6533

THAI

Hours:	Mon-Sat 11:00 a.m. to 3:00 p.m.,
	5:00 p.m. to 10:00 p.m.
	Sun 5:00 p.m. to 10:00 p.m.
Payment:	Credit cards
Parking:	Moderately difficult street parking
Atmosphere:	Casual, mid-scale, outside dining

Abundant possibilities exist here for both vegetarians and vegans. We love the Tom Kha (lemon mushroom soup), the Pak Kiew Waan (spicy green curry with vegetables, tofu, and basil), and Pad Ke-Mow ("drunken" noodles with broccoli, basil, and a spicy red sauce). But all of the vegetable curries are excellent and green beans with onions and mushrooms in a smoked chile sauce is exceptional.

VEGETARIAN FRIENDLY

★★/$
3. The Cool Café

328 Lomita Drive (in the Cantor Arts Center)
Stanford University, CA
650.725.4758

CALIFORNIAN

Hours:	*Wed, Fri-Sun 11:00 a.m. to 5:00 p.m.*
	Th 11:00 a.m. to 8:00 p.m.
	Closed Mon-Tue
Payment:	*Credit cards*
Parking:	*Moderate on-campus parking*
Atmosphere:	*Casual*

One of three restaurants founded by Jesse Cool, The Cool Café offers its organic fare to Stanford students, staff, faculty, and visitors. The food is substantially superior to what is available on many campuses. Vegetarians have a lot of choices here, from soups, beet salads, and bruschetta to egg salad sandwiches, grilled eggplant with spinach, and organic bananas, honey, chiles, and peanut butter on toast. The night menu always has a vegetarian entrée, but there is not much for vegans. Dairy products, coffee, and produce are almost all organic from sustainable sources.

VEGETARIAN FRIENDLY

★★/$
4. Crepevine

1310 Burlingame Avenue (at Park Road)
Burlingame, CA
650.344.1310

MIDDLE EASTERN CREPERY

Hours:	Sun-Th 7:30 a.m. to 11:00 p.m.
	Fri-Sat 7:30 a.m. to midnight
Payment:	Cash and local checks only
Parking:	Moderate street parking
Atmosphere:	Casual, lively

This place is often mistakenly identified as a vegetarian restaurant, but it isn't. You'll find poultry, beef, pork, and seafood among the selections. There are, however, plenty of choices for both vegans and vegetarians. In addition to fairly standard California-Mediterranean sandwiches, salads, and pastas, there are about a dozen egg dishes, a tofu scramble with mushrooms and spinach, and a lot of crepes. For crepes, we like Le Delice (cheddar cheese with glazed onions) and Greek (spinach, olives, almonds, onions, and feta cheese with cucumber yogurt sauce). Sweet crepes include one with Nutella and bananas. You can, if you prefer, create your own combinations. Anyone for Nutella and tofu?

VEGETARIAN FRIENDLY

★★★/$$$
5. Flea Street Cafe

3607 Alameda de las Pulgas
Menlo Park, CA
650.854.1226

CALIFORNIAN

Hours:	Tue-Sat 5:30 p.m. to 9:00 p.m.
	Sun 10:00 a.m. to 2:00 p.m.,
	5:30 p.m. to 8:00 p.m.
Payment:	Credit cards
Parking:	Free lot
Atmosphere:	Casual, mid-scale

Jesse Cool and her Flea Street Cafe are something of an institution in these parts. Cool often sports hot pink or turquoise stripes (and sometimes both) in her strawberry blonde hair and she is quick with her opinions, especially those having to do with her commitment to the organic, seasonal, and sustainable foods that form the core of her cuisine. As it must, the menu changes frequently to follow what is available on the farm, in the pasture, and in the nearby Pacific Ocean. Vegetarians will find plenty to enjoy here, from an early winter vegetable fritto misto with Meyer lemons and spicy aioli to local goat cheese in a pistachio crust served with arugula, beets-and-caper vinaigrette, and a mushroom and goat cheese Wellington.

VEGETARIAN FRIENDLY

★★/$$
6. Joy Meadow Restaurant

701 El Camino Real (near Brewster Street)
Redwood City, CA
650.780.9978

ASIAN

Hours:	*Daily 11:30 a.m. to 9:30 p.m.*
Payment:	*Credit cards*
Parking:	*Moderately difficult street parking, public lots nearby*
Atmosphere:	*Quiet, elegant, outdoor dining*

There are enough vegetarian entrées here—
most of them vegan—that it is easy to ignore
the nearly equal number that feature fish or
chicken. Clearly, vegetables are much more than
an afterthought. Entrées all have clever names,
like Bag of Fortune (a pouch of dough filled
with tofu, mushrooms, zucchini, carrots, and
water chestnuts served with a ginger-garlic
sauce), Cupid's Delight (crisped heart-shaped
pastry layered with marinated tofu, tomatoes,
cheese, cucumbers, and basil with a hoisin and
orange sauce), and Zen Banquet (mashed pota-
toes stuffed with vegetables and shaped like
pears). Joy Meadow is part of an urban sanctu-
ary that includes the Temple of Light, a non-
denominational spiritual center, and Angel of
Light Books and Gifts.

VEGETARIAN FRIENDLY

★★/$
7. jZCool Eatery & Catering Co.

827 Santa Cruz Avenue (near Evelyn Street)
Menlo Park, CA
650.325.2068

CALIFORNIAN

Hours:	*Sun-Mon 9:00 a.m. to 3:00 p.m.*
	Tue-Sat 11:00 a.m. to 8:00 p.m.
Payment:	*Credit cards*
Parking:	*Moderately difficult street parking*
Atmosphere:	*Very casual*

Portobello burgers, eggplant Parmigiano sandwiches, and veggie melts with ricotta are among
the vegetarian options at Jesse Cool's most casual
eatery. You can also try the simple grilled cheese
and peanut butter and jelly.

VEGETARIAN FRIENDLY

★★★★/$$$
8. Stoa Restaurant & Bar

3750 Fabian Way (at Charleston Road)
Palo Alto, CA
650.424.3900

CALIFORNIAN

Hours, restaurant:

Tue-Fri 11:30 a.m. to 3:00 p.m.,
5:30 p.m. to 10:30 p.m.
Sat-Sun 5:30 p.m. to 10:30 p.m.
Closed Mon

Hours, wine bar:

Tue-Th 11:30 a.m. to midnight
Fri 11:30 a.m. to 1:00 a.m.
Sat 5:30 p.m. to 1:00 a.m.
Sun 11:00 a.m. to midnight
Closed Mon

Payment: Credit cards
Parking: Free lot
Atmosphere: Elegant

Stoa is an excellent expression of a new breed of vegetarian restaurant that is upmarket and sophisticated, a destination for anyone who enjoys great food rather than an oasis for folks with food issues, as many vegetarian restaurants have been over the years. There is much less mock meat here than at Millennium, which clearly is the grandfather of restaurants such as Stoa. Instead, vegetables and grains are crafted with care in pristine salads and irresistible appetizers. Entrées such as wild mushroom strudel, truffled spinach raviolis, and coconut tempura vegetables with lemon-garlic fries and chipotle aioli are delicious and indulgent, and a blue cheese souffle with braised endive is positively heavenly. Dishes that can be prepared for vegans are marked with a discreet V and they make up about one-half to two-thirds of the menu.

VEGETARIAN WITH MANY VEGAN OPTIONS

Santa Clara and Santa Cruz Counties

★★/$
1. Amarin Thai Cuisine

156 Castro Street (near West Evelyn Avenue)
Mountain View, CA
650.988.9323

THAI

Hours:	*Mon-Th 11:00 a.m. to 3:00 p.m.,*
	5:00 p.m. to 10:00 p.m.
	Sat-Sun noon to 10:00 p.m.
	Closed Fri
Payment:	*Credit cards*
Parking:	*Free lot*
Atmosphere:	*Mid-scale, elegant, colorful*

Although not a vegetarian restaurant, Amarin Thai's menu offers forty-eight choices for vegetarians, many of them vegan. Fried taro, spicy corn cakes, bean thread noodle salad, eggplant salad, and shredded green papaya salad are excellent starters. Green curry with tofu and bamboo shoots is rich, luscious, and pleasantly spicy. Cabbage successfully takes the place of chicken in traditional coconut milk soup.

VEGETARIAN FRIENDLY

★/$$
2. China Wok

2633 California Street (near San Antonio Road)
Mountain View, CA
650.941.4373

CHINESE

Hours:	Mon-Fri 11:00 a.m. to 10:00 p.m.
	Sat-Sun noon to 10:00 p.m.
Payment:	Credit cards (no AmEx)
Parking:	Free lot
Atmosphere:	Dark, moody, mid-scale

Although China Wok is often included in listings of vegetarian-friendly restaurants in the Bay Area, only a small number of the dozens of listings actually are vegetarian and those are pretty standard: stir-fried vegetables over rice, broccoli in garlic sauce over rice, and the like. Assorted vegetables in a clay pot, mu shu vegetables, tofu in spicy secret sauce, and one vegetarian family dinner are the most interesting options.

VEGETARIAN FRIENDLY

★★★/$
3. Dasaprakash

2636 Homestead Road (near Layton Street)
Santa Clara, CA
408.246.8292

SOUTH INDIAN

Hours:	Mon-Fri 11:30 a.m. to 2:30 p.m.,
	5:30 p.m. to 10:00 p.m.
	Sat-Sun 11:30 a.m. to 10:00 p.m.
Payment:	Credit cards
Parking:	Moderately difficult street parking
Atmosphere:	Elegant, mid-scale, friendly

Fermented dumplings, dosas with a half dozen different fillings, lentil cakes, steamed rice cakes, lentil pancake with onions, lentil doughnut, stuffed potato patties, pakoras stuffed with apples, poories, and chapathi are excellent here. The pancakes are some of the yummiest around (we are especially fond of the one with onions, green chiles, and ginger). You'll also find intriguing rice dishes that go beyond the usual biryanis; desserts that feature everything from carrots to pineapple and rice; excellent ice creams; and good Indian beverages. Breakfast and lunch offer set menus; dinner is a la carte.

VEGETARIAN

★/$
4. Dee Dee's Indian Fast Food

2557 West Middlefield Road
  (near San Antonio Road)
Mountain View, CA
650.967.9333

INDIAN

Hours:	Daily 11:00 a.m. to 8:30 p.m.
Payment:	Credit cards
Parking:	Free lot
Atmosphere:	Very casual, in-store fast food

You'll find all the classics here, from biryanis to curries, samosas, and pakoras of every stripe. Because everything here is vegetarian, you don't even need to understand what a dish is (many of the dishes are listed by the Indian name only) to be able to try it. We particularly like lemon rice, peas, and carrot pulav, as well as buttermilk kadhi. Entrées change daily, and party platters (two appetizers, two entrées, daal, rice, bread, dessert, raita, and pickle) are $9.95 a person. Dee Dee's is also an Indian grocery.

VEGETARIAN

★★/$
5. Dharmas Natural Foods

4250 Capitola Road (near 41st Avenue)
Capitola, CA
831.462.1717

INTERNATIONAL

Hours:	*Daily 8:00 a.m. to 9:00 p.m.*
Payment:	*Cash only*
Parking:	*Free lot*
Atmosphere:	*Casual, eclectic, alternative*

Although you'll find a mix of Mediterranean, American, and Asian cuisines here, Mexican fare is at the heart of the offerings, with vegetarian and vegan versions of quesadillas, burritos, nachos, tacos, and chips with salsa. Add to this biscuits and gravy (vegan), Greek pasta, macaroni and cheese (vegan), lasagne (vegan), miso soup, chow mein, chili, cornbread, a tempeh reuben, and vegetarian burgers and hot dogs, and you pretty much have something for everyone. Omnivores will do best avoiding the faux meats but vegans will thrill at the possibilities for satisfying lingering cravings offered here. (A bit of trivia: Dharmas originally called itself McDharmas; McDonald's has sued the little place twice.)

VEGETARIAN

★★/$
6. El Camino Bueno Bueno Burritoria

2500 B El Camino Real (near Showers Drive)
Mountain View, CA
650.941.0220

MEXICAN-AMERICAN

Hours:	Mon-Fri 10:00 a.m. to 10:00 p.m.
	Sat 11:00 a.m. to 10:00 p.m.
	Sun 11:00 a.m. to 9:30 p.m.
Payment:	Credit cards (no AmEx)
Parking:	Free lot
Atmosphere:	Very casual, often crowded

It can be difficult to get a satisfying vegetarian meal at a traditional Mexican restaurant, and even more difficult for the vegan because meat, seafood, and cheese are crucial in so many dishes. Yet in California, there are an increasing number of Mexican-inspired eateries, such as Bueno Bueno, that offer good choices that echo some of the flavors of the classic cuisine. Here, nachos are made with real cheese (not that strange orange cheese-like sauce) and there are several burritos (a regular veggie, a super veggie, a regular vegan, and the ultimate veggie—which is vegan). Salsas, guacamole, and all sauces are made using fresh ingredients.

VEGETARIAN FRIENDLY

★/$$
7. Garden Fresh Restaurant

1245 West El Camino Real
  (near Miramonte Avenue)
Mountain View, CA
650.961.7795

INDIAN

Hours:	*Sun-Th 11:00 a.m. to 9:30 p.m.*
	Fri-Sat 11:00 a.m. to 10:00 p.m.
Payment:	*Credit cards (no AmEx)*
Parking:	*Free lot*
Atmosphere:	*Casual*

Garden Fresh takes faux meat to a new level
with its vegetarian kidneys (little nuggets of
wheat gluten fried until crunchy and tossed
with vegetables and basil). Also interesting is
fried tofu skin with brown sauce, corn and tofu
chowder, and curry noodle soup. As an appetizer,
try the taro spring rolls or basil mu shu "pork."

VEGAN

★★/$
8. Kokila Kitchen

20956 Homestead Road (near Stelling Street)
Cupertino, CA
408.777.8198

INDIAN (GUJARATI)

Hours:	Tue-Sun 11:00 a.m. to 2:00 p.m.,
	6:00 p.m. to 9:00 p.m.
	Closed Mon
Payment:	Credit cards (no AmEx)
Parking:	Free lot
Atmosphere:	Casual, homey

The South Bay is home to dozens of good Indian restaurants (a result of the large number of Indian immigrants who arrived to work in the high-tech industry), though few of them are strictly vegetarian or as good as Kokila. Vegetable biryani, chapati, garlic naan, and mutter paneer (fresh peas with homemade cheese) are among our favorite dishes. The structure of service here is unusual and understanding it is the only way to get the most out of it. Without advance reservations, your only option is a buffet, where the foods of Gujarati are rotated throughout the week. Yet if you call ahead, you can order other dishes to enjoy at the restaurant or take with you. After a few visits to the buffet, you might want to note your favorite items, then call before you return so that you can be sure to enjoy them again. However you choose to enjoy this treasure, don't miss the undhiyu, a nine-vegetable stew that must be ordered in advance.

VEGAN

★★/$
9. Komala Vilas

1020 East El Camino Real (at Henderson)
Sunnyvale, CA
408.733.7400

SOUTH INDIAN

Hours:	Sun-Mon, Wed-Sat
	8:30 a.m. to 10:30 a.m.,
	11:30 a.m. to 2:30 p.m.,
	7:00 p.m. to 9:00 p.m.
	Closed Tue
Payment:	Credit cards (no AmEx)
Parking:	Free lot
Atmosphere:	Elegant, mid-scale, clean

Indian dumplings, dosas, fried lentil cakes, and pongal made with rice and lentils are among the specialties popular with students in the area who flock to this family-operated restaurant. Masala dosa, filled with potatoes, onions, peas, and curry leaves, is among the best selections. At night, service is standard order-off-the-menu. Other meals feature fixed menus: breakfast ($5) and lunch ($8).

VEGETARIAN

★★★/$$$
10. La Fondue

14510 Big Basin Way (near 3rd Street)
Saratoga, CA
408.867.3332

FONDUE

Hours:	Mon-Th 5:00 p.m. to 9:30 p.m.
	Fri 4:45 p.m. to 11:00 p.m.
	Sat 3:15 p.m. to 11:00 p.m.
	Sun 3:45 p.m. to 9:30 p.m.
Payment:	Credit cards
Parking:	Easy
Atmosphere:	Elegant, mid-scale

Here, F stands for both fondue and fun, as guests spear morsels of food and swirl them in little cauldrons of broth, wine, sake, bubbling oil, or cheese. And if the retro meal—hugely popular in the 1960s and early 1970s—isn't enough nostalgia for you, the rules of fondue might just be a bit too much: If a woman loses her cube of bread in the common pot, we are told, she pays with a kiss to the man on her right. If a man loses a morsel, he pays by buying the next round of drinks. Vegetarians and vegans will want to shield their eyes from Wild Things, one of several full fondue dinners for two, and focus instead on garden vegetables, wild mushrooms, tofu, and, for dessert, tantalizing chocolate fondue. A great indulgence, perfect for a romantic evening.

VEGETARIAN FRIENDLY

★★/$
11. Lu Lai Garden

> 210 Barber Court (near McCarthy Boulevard)
> Milpitas, CA
> 408.526.9888

CHINESE

Hours:	Daily 10:30 a.m. to 2:30 p.m.,
	5:00 p.m. to 9:15 p.m.
Payment:	Cash and local checks only
Parking:	Free lot
Atmosphere:	Casual, mid-scale noodle joint

If you're a fan of Asian noodles, you'll find plenty here—boiled, pan-fried, and simmered in soups. Pickled mustard chow mein, rice noodles with shredded vegetables, Singapore-style rice noodles, and mushroom noodle soup are among our favorites. If you're craving duck or chicken, you'll find satisfying mock versions in noodle and rice dishes. You'll also find several versions of rice porridge—also known as congee and jook—a supremely satisfying dish that is often served in Asia for breakfast or as an after-the-bars 3:00 a.m. snack. Several dessert soups round out the menu.

VEGETARIAN

★★/$
12. Milan Sweet Center

296 South Abel Street (near Serra Way)
Milpitas, CA
408.946.2525

INDIAN

Hours:	Mon 10:00 a.m. to 2:30 p.m.
	Tue-Th 10:00 a.m. to 8:00 p.m.
	Fri-Sat 10:00 a.m. to 9:00 p.m.
	Sun 10:00 a.m. to 8:00 p.m.
Payment:	Credit cards (no AmEx)
Parking:	Easy street parking
Atmosphere:	Casual, fast food

Don't let the name fool you: This is not a northern Italian dessert shop. Rather, it's a popular Indian snack shack, with veggie burgers, tandoori pizza (weekends only), dosas, samosa, pakoras, and, yes, a lot of Indian sweets. Much of the business here is take-out and catering. Many of several dozen menu items may be unfamiliar but you can relax when it comes to meat: Milan Sweet Center is entirely vegetarian. Vegans will need to inquire about specific items.

VEGETARIAN

★★/$

13. Noodle King

2455 South Winchester Boulevard
  (near Kennedy Avenue)
Campbell, CA
408.374.9791

VIETNAMESE & CHINESE

Hours:	Tue-Sun 11:00 a.m. to 3:00 p.m.,
	5:00 p.m. to 9:00 p.m.
	Closed Mon
Payment:	Credit cards
Parking:	Free lot
Atmosphere:	Casual

Restaurants that combine Vietnamese fare with
one or more styles of Chinese cuisine are
increasingly popular. Here, most of the selections involve seafood, poultry, or meat but there
is a vegetarian section on the menu and several
of the other dishes can be made vegetarian on
request. Spicy eggplant hot pot, onion with
mixed vegetables, and salted black beans with
tofu are some of the better choices. Noodle King
also offers rice porridge (known as congee and
jook as well), but you'll have to request a vegetarian version, as none is listed on the menu.

VEGETARIAN FRIENDLY

★★/$$
14. Passage to India

1100 West El Camino Real (at Oak Street)
Mountain View, CA
650.964.5532

INDIAN

Hours:	*Daily 11:30 a.m. to 2:30 p.m.,*
	5:00 p.m. to 10:00 p.m.
Payment:	*Credit cards*
Parking:	*Free lot*
Atmosphere:	*Elegant, mid-scale*

In addition to about a dozen vegetarian entrées, the diversity of fresh Indian breads here will ensure than any vegetarian is well fed. Try the pan-fried aloo paratha (a pan-fried flat bread stuffed with potatoes), or the wonderful onion kulcha (naan stuffed with onions). Nearly a dozen tempting dosas, vegetarian biryani, and chana masala are good choices, and be sure to order raita, a condiment of yogurt and cucumbers, to accompany them or just about anything else. There are lunch and dinner buffets daily and a brunch buffet on weekends. Passage to India offers excellent take-out service, too.

VEGETARIAN FRIENDLY

★★★/$
15. Saravana Bhavan

600 West El Camino Real (near Lane Avenue)
Mountain View, CA
650.625.0460

INDIAN

Hours:	Tue-Th 11:30 a.m. to 2:00 p.m.,
	5:30 p.m. to 10:00 p.m.
	Fri-Sat 11:00 a.m. to 3:00 p.m.,
	5:30 p.m. to 10:30 p.m.
	Sun 11:00 a.m. to 3:00 p.m.,
	5:30 p.m. to 10:30 p.m.
	Closed Mon
Payment:	Credit cards (no AmEx)
Parking:	Easy street parking
Atmosphere:	Mid-scale urban diner

There's a good chance we'll be seeing more branches of Saravana Bhavan in the Bay Area and beyond. The company, founded in India about twenty-two years ago by a high-school dropout with a passion for success, has locations in India, Dubai, and Malaysia. And judging from the popularity of this first American location, more seem likely. The food is fresh, authentic, diverse, and delicious, with a variety of flat breads with yummy condiments for dipping. Dosas are excellent, as is the coconut chutney and a puree of fresh cilantro. And try the milk tea; it is both authentic and satisfying, as only the real thing can be.

VEGETARIAN

★★/$
16. Shoreline Bueno Bueno Burritoria

1477 C Plymouth Street (off Shoreline Boulevard,
   east of Highway 101)
Mountain View, CA
650.962.9079

MEXICAN-AMERICAN

Hours:	*Mon-Fri 10:30 a.m. to 5:00 p.m.*
	Closed Sat-Sun
Payment:	*Credit cards (no AmEx)*
Parking:	*Free lot*
Atmosphere:	*Very casual, often crowded*

It can be difficult to get a satisfying vegetarian meal at a traditional Mexican restaurant, and even more difficult for the vegan because meat, seafood, and cheese are crucial in so many dishes. Yet in California, there are an increasing number of Mexican-inspired eateries, such as Bueno Bueno, that offer good choices that echo some of the flavors of the classic cuisine. Here, nachos are made with real cheese (not that strange orange cheese-like sauce) and there are several burritos (a regular veggie, a super veggie, a regular vegan, and the ultimate veggie—which is vegan). Salsas, guacamole, and all sauces are made using fresh ingredients.

VEGETARIAN FRIENDLY

★★/$$
17. Sue's Indian

216 Castro Street (near Villa Street)
Mountain View, CA
650.969.1112

INDIAN

Hours:	Daily 11:00 a.m. to 2:30 p.m.,
	5:00 p.m. to 10:00 p.m.
Payment:	Credit cards (no AmEx)
Parking:	Difficult street parking
Atmosphere:	Casual, mid-scale

Although founder Sue Sista died in 2001, her finely crafted cuisine lives on at the restaurant that bears her name. Numerous vegetarian selections reflect the popularity of the diet in India. In addition to the usual roundup (cauliflower and potato curry, curried garbanzo beans, and vegetable biryani), there are several less familiar selections, such as stewed okra, fermented rice and lentil cakes, tandoori eggplant, vegetable vindaloo, and several tasty dosas.

VEGETARIAN FRIENDLY

★★/$
18. Udupi Palace

> 976 East El Camino Real (near Poplar Avenue)
> Sunnyvale, CA
> 408.830.9600

SOUTH INDIAN

Hours:	Daily 11:30 a.m. to 10:30 p.m.
Payment:	Credit cards
Parking:	Moderately difficult street parking
Atmosphere:	Casual

Dosas—think spicy Indian crepes—are a signature at this popular place that now has three locations (Newark, Berkeley, and Sunnyvale). You can make a meal simply of dosas, as many people do; there is plenty of variety and they are delicious and satisfying. For a more diverse experience, Udupi Palace offers a special combo meal with daal, two curries, biryani, raita, chutney, rice pudding, papadam, and steamed white rice cake; it's the perfect way to go when you don't feel like thinking. There's mango lassi, and if you've ever been to India, you'll be thrilled by the coffee, which appears to be Nescafe in hot milk, a ubiquitous beverage at cafes on the subcontinent.

VEGETARIAN

Sonoma County

★★/$$
1. Annapurna Restaurant

535 Ross Street (between Mendocino and
B Streets)
Santa Rosa, CA
707.8579.8471

HIMALAYAN

Hours:	Mon-Sat 11:30 a.m. to 2:30 p.m.,
	5:00 p.m. to 9:30 p.m.
	Closed Sun
Payment:	Credit cards
Parking:	Moderate street parking
Atmosphere:	Casual, outside tables

"This reminds me of what we eat in the ashram,"
a colleague explained as we nestled on cushions
at the low tables of Annapurna, a friendly and
humble Himalayan restaurant on the edge of
downtown Santa Rosa. She was referring to an
ashram in upstate New York, where as chef she
presided over the preparation of about 10,000
vegetarian meals a day—so her opinion has
weight. Every day there is an all-you-can-eat
buffet with wonderful cauliflower and potato
curry, crunchy pakoras, and chewy naan scented
with garlic and cilantro. You cannot always tell
what is meat and what isn't, so be sure to ask;
the place is very popular with vegetarians so the
kitchen is clearly accommodating. Chana masala,
a garbanzo bean curry in a fragrant sauce redo-
lent with ginger and garlic, is glorious, perhaps
the best thing on the menu. The dinner menu
includes a combination vegetarian meal, so you
don't even have to think if you don't feel like it.
Masala tea is excellent.

VEGETARIAN FRIENDLY

★★/$
2. Chai Baba Chai

463 Sebastopol Avenue (at Bosley Street)
Santa Rosa, CA
707.544.2222

INTERNATIONAL

Hours:	Wed-Sat 11:00 a.m. to 3:00 p.m., 5:00 p.m. to 7:30 p.m.
	Sun 11:00 a.m. to 3:00 p.m.
	Closed Mon-Tue
Payment:	Cash, local checks
Parking:	Easy street parking
Atmosphere:	Very small, casual

The miniscule size of this earnest cafe encourages takeout, though the food here is best when enjoyed right out of the kitchen. It's hard to reheat a veggie burger successfully, and it is the veggie burger—here called Baba's Love Burger, after the owner, Rich Love—that is the house specialty. Made of lentils, brown rice, oats, hemp seed, flax seed, walnuts, and a variety of vegetables, it's about as good as a veggie burger gets. Vegetable salads with beets and avocado, roasted potatoes with aioli, Asian-style cole slaw, tabbouleh (which would be better without the carrots), and a falafel sandwich are among the best offerings here. Avoid the pesto pizza (actually, avoid all pesto pizzas unless the pesto is added after cooking), and for dessert, consider the fruit salad spiked with orange flower water.

VEGAN

★★★/$$
3. Cucina Paradiso

> 56 East Washington Street (in the Golden Eagle
>   Center, near Water Street)
> Petaluma, CA
> 707.782.1130

ITALIAN

Hours:	Mon-Th 11:30 a.m. to 2:30 p.m.,
	5:00 p.m. to 9:00 p.m.
	Fri-Sat 11:30 a.m. to 2:30 p.m.,
	5:00 p.m. to 10:00 p.m.
	Closed Sun
Payment:	Credit cards
Parking:	Large free lot
Atmosphere:	Dark, elegant, mid-scale

Italians have a wonderful way with vegetables
and you don't need to find a vegetarian restau-
rant to enjoy them. Cucina Paradiso is one of
those hidden-in-plain-sight gems, offering a
number of excellent options for nonmeat-eaters.
If you ask your server to hold the smoked
salmon, you can just about make a meal of the
antipasti, which includes grilled eggplant,
asparagus, and zucchini; roasted peppers; tomato
topped with mozzarella; and two bruschetta,
one with chopped tomatoes and basil and one
with an addictive smear of black truffle puree.
Salads are good and tomato bread soup is per-
haps the best version in the known universe.
Potato gnocchi with Gorgonzola and walnuts is
rich and satisfying without being heavy, and
porcini ravioli in butter and sage sauce is deli-
cate and delicious.

VEGETARIAN FRIENDLY

★★★★/$$
4. Dempsey's Restaurant and Brewery

50 East Washington Street (in the Golden Eagle
Shopping Center)
Petaluma, CA
707.765.9694

CALIFORNIAN

Hours:	*Mon-Wed, Sun 11:30 a.m. to 9:00 p.m.*
	Thu, Sat 11:30 a.m. to 9:30 p.m.
	Fri 11:30 a.m. to 10:00 p.m.
Payment:	*Credit cards*
Parking:	*Large free lot*
Atmosphere:	*Lively brew pub, outside dining*

Dempsey's offers some of the finest food in the Bay Area and their beers and ales are outstanding, too. There are always several vegetarian dishes and many are made with fruits and vegetables picked the same morning at the restaurant's organic farm, Red Rooster Ranch, where owners Peter and Bernadette Burrell live with their children. Selections change almost daily, as you would expect from a place so connected to the land. Among the dishes you will find are artisan cheeses roasted in the wood oven and served with grilled vegetables, roasted red onions, and flat bread; fresh farm greens with roasted pears, onions, goat cheese, and almond vinaigrette; Red Rooster Pizza with mozzarella, just-harvested tomatoes, and hand-picked basil; and butternut squash layered with garlicky chard, roasted onions, and spicy pipian sauce. Bernadette's bread-and-butter pickles are addictive. Pub food just doesn't get any better than this.

VEGETARIAN FRIENDLY

★★★★/$$
5. Downtown Bakery & Creamery

308 Center Street (near Matheson Street)
Healdsburg, CA
707.431.2719

BAKERY & CREAMERY

Hours:	Mon-Fri 6:00 a.m. to 5:30 p.m.
	Sat 7:00 a.m. to 5:30 p.m.
	Sun 7:00 a.m. to 4:00 p.m.
Payment:	Credit cards
Parking:	Moderate street parking
Atmosphere:	Takeout only

If you find yourself in Healdsburg, this is an excellent place to stop for refueling. The breads are outstanding; the desserts, gelatos, and ice creams phenomenal; and there is full coffee and tea service. The sweet little place is also a nexus of community where you are assured of running into friends with the latest news. Everything here is made from scratch, using top ingredients like local eggs, butter, cream, and organic fruit at the peak of its season. You'll find breakfast pastries such as sticky buns, fruit turnovers, and pain du chocolat; at lunch, there are sandwiches, pizzas, focaccia by the slice, and flat bread pizzettas. Galettes—free-form tarts filled with fresh fruit—are among the best desserts in the North Bay. Downtown Bakery & Creamery offers holiday desserts and, by special order, wedding cakes and cakes for other special occasions; the desserts and cakes are delicious, gorgeous, and sophisticated. House-made doughs, such as puff pastry, galette dough, pie dough, and cookie dough are available for the home cook.

VEGETARIAN FRIENDLY

★/$$
6. East West Bakery & Cafe

2323 Sonoma Avenue (near Farmers Lane)
Santa Rosa, CA
707.546.6142

INTERNATIONAL

Hours:	Tue-Sun 8:00 a.m. to 9:00 p.m.
	Closed Mon
Payment:	Credit cards (no AmEx)
Parking:	Easy street parking
Atmosphere:	Casual, counter service

See next page for details.

VEGETARIAN FRIENDLY

★/$$
7. East West Bakery & Cafe

128 North Main Street (near Highway 12)
Sebastopol, CA
707.829.2822

INTERNATIONAL

Hours:	Sun-Th 8:00 a.m. to 8:00 p.m.
	Fri-Sat 8:00 a.m. to 9:00 p.m.
Payment:	Credit cards
Parking:	Moderately difficult street parking, free public lots nearby
Atmosphere:	Casual, counter service

Although East West calls its cuisine international vegetarian, there's plenty of animal flesh on the menu. Interestingly, it does not seem to scare away committed vegetarians, who have always been partial to this place. For breakfast, pancakes are excellent. When lentil stew with pomegranates is available, get it; it is outstanding. Some dishes can be greasy and others can be heavy—much like California hippie cuisine in the 1970s—so stick with salads, Middle Eastern appetizers, and lighter fare and you'll do fine.

VEGETARIAN FRIENDLY

★★/$$
8. Govinda's

2765 Yulupa Avenue (near Bethards Drive)
Santa Rosa, CA
707.544.2491

INTERNATIONAL

Hours:	Mon-Fri 11:30 a.m. to 2:30 p.m.,
	5:00 p.m. to 8:00 p.m.
	Sat 5:00 p.m. to 8:00 p.m.
	Closed Sun
Payment:	Credit cards
Parking:	Free lot
Atmosphere:	Casual, buffet

The core offerings here are Indian, and the style of service—an all-you-can-eat buffet—reflects the lunch buffets popular in many Indian restaurants. But unlike Indian restaurants, Govinda's offers dark, sweet cornbread, an American-style salad bar, pasta, chili, and brown rice. There's tender lasagne with plenty of cheese, traditional daal, and vegetable curries. The lack of culinary focus can make it difficult to pull together a cohesive meal, especially for the novice diner, but because you can return to the buffet as many times as you like (though you are encouraged to eat all you take), we suggest eating in several courses rather than piling your plate with too many conflicting dishes. If you want pasta with California hippie-style marinara sauce (with vegetables, which are not traditional), enjoy it alone or with salad. If you want curry, accompany it with rice and daal, not pasta.

VEGETARIAN

★★★/$$
9. JhanThong Banbua

2400 Mendocino Avenue (near Steele Lane)
Santa Rosa, CA
707.528.8048

THAI

Hours:	Mon-Fri 11:00 a.m. to 3:00 p.m., 5:00 p.m. to 10:00 p.m.
	Sat 5:00 p.m. to 10:00 p.m.
	Closed Sun
Payment:	Credit cards (no AmEx)
Parking:	Small free lot
Atmosphere:	Elegant, mid-scale

One of the best Thai restaurants in the entire Bay Area, JhanThong Banbua offers a choice of meat, seafood, or vegetables in all curries, nearly all entrées, and most appetizers. Everything is good. For a light lunch, try the fresh salad rolls with noodles, julienned vegetables, and sweet-hot plum sauce for dipping. Steamed spinach with peanut sauce is outstanding and poaug tod (deep-fried balls of tarot root, a sometimes bland dish) are zesty and flavorful in their crunchy batter. Meaing Lao, one of several variations of lettuce wrap, comes with crispy rice, toasted coconut, peanuts, ginger, shallots, tiny lime wedges, marinated turnip, and tangy soy-based sauce; as do all the other versions, it explodes in the mouth in a grand symphony of flavors.

VEGETARIAN FRIENDLY

★★★★/$$
10. Jimtown Store

6706 State Highway 128 (Alexander Valley Road)
Healdsburg, CA
707.433.1212

CALIFORNIAN

Hours:	Mon-Fri 7:00 a.m. to 5:00 p.m.
	Sat-Sun 7:30 a.m. to 5:00 p.m.
Payment:	Credit cards
Parking:	Free lot
Atmosphere:	Rustic

Jimtown Store is a little country market with a big reputation and a long history: It opened in 1893 and has been profiled in the *New Yorker*, the *New York Times*, and many other publications. The store, operated today by the amazingly charming Carrie Brown, is a delightful mix of toys from the 1950s and 1960s, antiques, housewares, local wines, and books by local authors, including Carrie Brown. One of the most important elements of Jimtown is its food, sold mostly as take-out though there are a few tables and chairs and a couple of counters should you want to eat in. Boxed lunches are perfect to take wine tasting or sightseeing, and boxed dinners are good for locals who want a night off from cooking and for visitors passing through or staying at one of the area's many bed and breakfast inns. Though not vegetarian, there are excellent options, such as Jimtown's famous olive-and-fig tapenade smeared on a baguette, without or without goat cheese, and an eggplant sandwich with Jimtown's house-made roasted vegetable spread. Salads include Carrie's mom's potato salad, melonseed pasta salad with roasted vegetables, and wild rice salad with pomegranate vinaigrette.

VEGETARIAN FRIENDLY

★★★★/$$

11. K & L Bistro

119 Main Street (near Bodega Avenue)
Sebastopol, CA
707.823.6614

FRENCH

Hours:	Tue-Sat 11:30 a.m. to 3:00 p.m.,
	5:00 p.m. to 10:00 p.m.
	Closed Sun-Mon
Payment:	Credit cards
Parking:	Moderately difficult street parking
Atmosphere:	Elegant, mid-scale

Some of the best vegetarian dishes I've had any-
where have been at this charming little bistro.
When a committed vegetarian found nothing on
the menu that met her requirements, the
kitchen quickly offered two suggestions: pasta
primavera and risotto with artichokes and
asparagus. We both had the risotto, which was
extraordinary. The options for vegetarians and
vegans are limited, but what there is will be
excellent. Sometimes you'll find an interesting
celery dish on the menu, a rare treat as few con-
temporary chefs feature celery as a centerpiece.
The frites are state-of-the-art; ask for a side of
aioli for dipping.

VEGETARIAN FRIENDLY

★/$$
12. Mystic Isle Cafe

10400 Highway 1 (near Highway 116)
Jenner, CA
707.865.2233

CALIFORNIAN

Hours:	Th-Sun 8:00 a.m. to 2:00 p.m.,
	5:00 p.m. to 9:00 p.m.
	Closed Mon-Wed
Payment:	Credit cards
Parking:	Small lot
Atmosphere:	Elegant, mid-scale

The Mystic Isle Cafe is one of a handful of restaurants in the charming hamlet of Jenner, where the Russian River merges with the Pacific Ocean. For years, Sizzling Tandoor, just south of the bridge over the river, has offered the best choices for vegetarians, but Mystic River Cafe presents several options, too. You'll find vegetarian spring rolls, puff pastry filled with a mélange of vegetables and tofu, and vegan Asian-style stir-fries served over basmati rice. There are always several vegetable side dishes, too. However, many of the dishes are curiously sweet when they should be savory. Still, the room is gorgeous and it's a great place for a slow, romantic dinner, especially if new love has quelled your appetite.

VEGETARIAN FRIENDLY

★★★/$

13. North Light Books and Cafe

550 East Cotati Avenue
   (in the Rancho Cotati Center)
Cotati, CA
707.792.4300

CALIFORNIAN

Hours:	*Mon-Fri 7:00 a.m. to 9:00 p.m.*
	Sat 8:00 a.m. to 7:00 p.m.
	Sun 9:00 a.m. to 6:00 p.m.
Payment:	*Credit cards*
Parking:	*Large free lot*
Atmosphere:	*In-store cafe, patio dining*

North Light is sweet and eclectic, with a book-store; a stage where readings and open mike take place weekly; a spacious patio where you can linger with friends, a book, or your iBook; and very good food. You often see the owners shopping at local farmers' markets. Sandwiches on pugliese smeared with tapenade, roasted peppers, and cheese; lusty salads; and daily specials keep students from nearby Sonoma State, local writers and artists, and neighbors coming back again and again. The menu changes daily, offering such tasty selections as goat cheese crepes, cheddar soup, tabbouleh, and all manner of sweets baked in-house. Breakfasts are good, too, with toast, French toast, oatmeal, omelets, and pastries. Good coffee drinks, hot apple cider, teas and wine, too.

VEGETARIAN FRIENDLY

★★★/$$
14. Seaweed Cafe

1580 Eastshore Road (at Highway 1)
Bodega Bay, CA
707.875.2700

CALIFORNIA-FRENCH

Hours:	Th-Mon 8:30 to 11:30 a.m. (breakfast)
	11:30 a.m. to 2:30 p.m. (lunch)
	Fri-Sat dinner (two seatings),
	5:30 p.m. and 7:30 p.m.
Payment:	Cash, checks, and credit cards
Parking:	Small parking lot
Atmosphere:	Charming, elegant, mid-scale

Seaweed Cafe offers some of the best food available on the Sonoma Coast, and though it is not vegetarian, Chef Jackie Martine works magic with vegetables, including sea vegetables. Salads sparkle like the night sky with an almost heart-breaking freshness, a cheese plate features the best of local artisan producers, and an earthy smoked pepper is scrumptious. Not for the vegan, but adventurous vegetarians will find much to enjoy here.

VEGETARIAN FRIENDLY

★★/$$
15. Sizzling Tandoor

9960 Highway One (at Highway 116)
Jenner, CA
707.865.0000

INDIAN

Hours:	Daily 11:30 a.m. to 3:00 p.m.,
	5:00 p.m. to 9:00 p.m.
	Closed Tue
Payment:	Credit cards
Parking:	Free lot
Atmosphere:	Casual, mid-scale

Although no longer the only place for a good meal on the Sonoma Coast (Seaweed Cafe has given a long-needed boost in quality to what is available here), Sizzling Tandoor remains one of the best choices for vegetarians. There are no unexpected dishes, but the naan is excellent, a trio of condiments (garbanzo bean sauce, tamarind sauce, and fresh cilantro-mint puree) delicious, and the vegetarian appetizers and entrées all that they should be. Tandoor-roasted eggplant, cauliflower, and potato curry, as well as fragrant pulao (basmati rice, vegetables, and nuts) are both outstanding. Vegetable samosas and pakoras are very good and a salad of potatoes and cucumbers in a slightly sweet dressing is wonderfully refreshing. The first location of Sizzling Tandoor in downtown Santa Rosa has not maintained the level of quality of the coastal restaurant; in recent years, the food there has been tired and disappointing.

VEGETARIAN FRIENDLY

★/$$
16. Slice of Life

6970 McKinley (near Main Street)
Sebastopol, CA
707.829.6627

INTERNATIONAL

Hours:	Tue-Fri 11:30 a.m. to 9:00 p.m.
	Sat 11:00 a.m. to 10:00 p.m.
	Sun 11:00 a.m. to 9:00 p.m.
	Closed Mon
Payment:	Cash, local checks
Parking:	Easy free lot, except during lunch hour
Atmosphere:	Casual diner

Slice of Life is a restaurant with a mission and they don't hesitate to let you know exactly what it is. The menu includes a heavy-handed serving of philosophy about diet, health, the environment, and world hunger. Should you request something deemed unworthy—a coke, for example, or real cheese instead of their usual soy cheese—expect a scolding and a lecture. You'll get the cheese, but there are no corporate sodas on the premises. Unsuspecting customers can find the approach humiliating—a simple "we don't have Coke" would suffice—but those who are passionate about their food politics flock to this little cafe. If you stick with salads and fresh vegetables, avoid the cloying mock meats, and go for real cheese, you can have a decent meal here, but many of the soy preparations have muddy flavors and unpleasant textures.

VEGAN

★★/$$
17. Sparks

16248 Main Street (near Church Street)
Guerneville, CA
707.869.8206

INTERNATIONAL

Hours:	Mon-Tue, Thu 11:00 a.m. to 2:00 p.m.
	Fri 11:00 a.m. to 2:00 p.m.,
	5:30 p.m. to 9:00 p.m.
	Sat-Sun 10:00 a.m. to 3:00 p.m.,
	5:30 p.m. to 9:00 p.m.
	Closed Wed
Payment:	Credit cards (no AmEx or Discover)
Parking:	East street parking, free lot
Atmosphere:	Casual, mid-scale

Sparks is very popular with the Sonoma County vegetarian crowd, especially since its move from Cotati to the heart of the Russian River. The menu is long on soy imitations of traditional fare (egg salad, feta cheese, corned beef, and turkey, to name a few faux favorites), all of which have an undertaste and a texture that becomes cloying after a few bites. Foods—such as roasted kabocha squash, black beans, avocados, and simple pastas—that are not trying to masquerade as something else tend to be better. The most interesting flourish here may be the menu's notation that it has been printed on paper made from recycled United States currency.

VEGAN

★★★/$$
18. Thai House

525 Fourth Street (between Mendocino Avenue
and B Street)
Santa Rosa, CA
707.526.3939

Thai

Hours:	Tue-Thu 11:30 a.m. to 3:00 p.m., 5:00 p.m. to 9:30 p.m.
	Fri-Sat 11:30 a.m. to 3:00 p.m., 5:00 p.m. to 10:00 p.m.
	Sun 5:00 p.m. to 9:30 p.m.
	Closed Mon
Payment:	Credit cards (no AmEx)
Parking:	Moderately difficult street parking, free and paid lots nearby
Atmosphere:	Elegant, mid-scale

For years, Thai House was situated about ten
miles south of Santa Rosa in Rohnert Park. Its
current location is centrally located but a bit
hard to find up a long flight of stairs and down
a hallway. You need to look up to see the sign,
which has a tendency to get lost amidst the
skateboarders, coffee houses, and retail shops
on this part of Fourth Street. But once inside,
you will be charmed by the light-filled space.
Everything here is good, so vegetarians should
simply search the menu for dishes that feature
vegetables and tofu, like the sublime pumpkin
curry with basil and spinach. If mangos are in
season, do not miss the sweet rice and mango
dessert, one of the best things you could possibly
eat anywhere, ever.

Vegetarian friendly

★★★★/$$
19. Water Street Bistro

100 Petaluma Boulevard North, Suite 106
  (at Western Avenue)
Petaluma, CA
707.763.9563

CALIFORNIA-FRENCH

Hours:	Mon-Fri 7:30 a.m. to 3:30 p.m.
	(4:00 p.m. after time change)
	Sat 8:00 a.m. to 4:00 p.m.
	Sun 8:30 a.m. to 2:30 p.m.
	Closed Tue
Payment:	Cash and checks
Parking:	Moderately difficult street parking
Atmosphere:	Tiny, charming, eclectic

This charming bistro belongs to the remarkably talented Stephanie Rastetter, who was the unsung hero of Babette's, a restaurant that since its closing has become almost mythical in the minds of those who either ate there or wished they had. Stephanie worked side by side with chef-owner Daniel Patterson, who closed Babette's and opened Elizabeth Daniel in San Francisco. Water Street Bistro has two things in common with Babette's: both were tiny and both were uncompromising in their commitment to top-notch ingredients and flawless techniques. But Babette's was formal; Water Street is casual. Two large white boards behind a curving counter list menu items and small black boards announce daily specials, wines, and other special beverages. For breakfast, you'll find buttermilk waffles, smoothies, house-made scones, cinnamon toast, and a selection of other scrumptious pastries. At lunch there is always a soup or two, always several specials, and always pickled black-eyed peas and chickpea salad with herb vinaigrette. A goat cheese and watercress sandwich is one of the best, most refreshing sandwiches around. Service will make you feel like a member of the family.

VEGETARIAN FRIENDLY

CERTIFIED FARMERS MARKETS

To support organic agriculture and sustainable farming, it is best to search for markets, farm stands, and other sources that are local, which is to say owned and controlled by members of the community and filled with foods, including fresh produce, from producers who live and work in the community. Think Globally, Eat Locally.

Alameda County

Alameda CFM
Taylor & Webster
Tuesdays, 9:30 a.m. to 1 p.m.
800.949.FARM

Berkeley Tuesday CFM
Derby & Martin Luther King
Tuesdays, 2 p.m. to 7 p.m.
510.548.3333

Pleasanton Tuesday CFM
W. Angela & Main
First Wednesdays, 5 p.m. to 9 p.m.
May through August
800.949.FARM

Berkeley Shattuck Organic CFM
Elephant Pharmacy Parking Lot
Shattuck, at Cedar
Thursdays, 2 p.m. to 6 p.m.
510.548.3333

Livermore CFM
Carnagie Park & 3rd & J
Thursdays, 4 p.m. to 8 p.m.
May through October
800.949.FARM

E. Oakland CFM
73rd Ave. & International Blvd.
Fridays, 10 a.m. to 2 p.m.
May through November
510.638.1742

Emeryville CFM
Bay St. & Shelmound
Fridays, 11 a.m. to 3 p.m.
June through October
415.382.7846

Oakland Kaiser CFM
Howe between MacArthur & 40th St.
Fridays, 10 a.m. to 2 p.m.
May through November
800.949.FARM

Old Oakland CFM
9th & Broadway
Fridays, 8 a.m. to 2 p.m.
510.745.7100

Berkeley Saturday CFM
Center St. & Martin Luther King
Saturdays, 10 a.m. to 3 p.m.
510.548.3333

Fremont Centerville CFM
Bonde & Fremont Blvd.
Saturdays, 9 a.m. to 1 p.m.
June through November
800.897.FARM

Hayward CFM
Main & B St.
Saturdays, 9 a.m. to 1 p.m.
800.897.FARM

Oakland Grand Lake CFM
Grand & Lakepark Way
Saturdays, 10 a.m. to 2 p.m.
800.897.FARM

Oakland Mandela CFM
5th St. & Mandela Parkway
Saturdays, 10 a.m. to 4 p.m.
510.776.4178

Oakland Millsmount CFM
MacArthur at Seminary
Saturdays, 10 a.m. to 2 p.m.
800.897.FARM

Pleasanton CFM
W. Angela & Main
Saturdays, 9 a.m. to 1 p.m.
800.949.FARM

San Leandro Bayfair Mall CFM
Fairmont & E. 14th—Bayfair Mall
Saturdays, 9 a.m to 1 p.m.
800.806.FARM

Union City-Old Alvarado CFM
Ceasar Chavez Park
Saturdays, 9 a.m. to 1 p.m.
May through November
800.949.FARM

Fremont Irvington CFM
Bay & Fremont Blvd.
Sundays, 9 a.m. to 1 p.m.
800.897.FARM

Oakland Jack London CFM
Broadway & Embarcadero
Sundays, 10 a.m. to 2 p.m.
800.949.FARM

Santa Clara Sunday CFM
Franklin & Monroe
Sundays, 9 a.m. to 1 p.m.
June through October
510.745.7100

Contra Costa County

Concord Tuesday CFM
Todo Santos Park
Willow Pass Road, at Grant Street
Tuesdays, 10 a.m. to 2 p.m.
800.949.FARM

El Cerrito CFM
El Cerrito Plaza
San Pablo Ave., at Fairmont Ave.
Tuesdays, 9 a.m. to 1 p.m.
510.528.7992

Concord Thursday CFM
Todo Santos Park
Willow Pass Rd., at Grant St.
Thursdays, 4 p.m. to 8 p.m.
May through October
800.949.FARM

Martinez CFM
Court & Main
Thursdays, 10 a.m. to 2 p.m.
May through November
800.949.FARM

Walnut Creek CFM
Bonanza St. & Locust
Thursdays, 4 p.m. to 8 p.m.
June through August
925.431.8361

Richmond CFM
Civic Center Plaza Dr. &
    McDonald Ave.
Fridays, 12 p.m. to 6 p.m.
May through November
510.758.2336

Walnut Creek Rossmore CFM
Rossmoor Clubhouse Parking Lot
Golden Rain Rd., at Rice
    Valley Rd.
Fridays, 9 a.m. to 11 a.m.
May through October
800.806.FARM

Danville CFM
Railroad & Prospect
Saturdays, 9 a.m. to 1 p.m.
800.949.FARM

El Cerrito CFM
El Cerrito Plaza
San Pablo Ave., at Fairmont Ave.
Saturdays, 9 a.m. to 1 p.m.
510.528.7992

Orinda CFM
Avenida de Orinda & Orinda Way
Saturdays, 9 a.m. to 1 p.m.
May through November
925.431.8361

Pinole CFM
Civic Center Parking Lot
Plum & Prune
Saturdays, 9 a.m. to 1 p.m.
May through November
800.949.FARM

Pleasant Hill CFM
Trelany Rd. Downtown—behind
    City Hall
Saturdays, 10 a.m. to 2 p.m.
May through October
925.431.8361

Martinez CFM
600 Block Main St., at
    Castro St.
Sundays, 10 a.m. to 2 p.m.
May through October
925.431.8361

Walnut Creek CFM
Broadway & Lincoln
Sundays, 8 a.m. to 1 p.m.
925.431.8361

Marin County

Novato Downtown CFM
Sherman & Grant
Tuesdays, 4 p.m. to 8 p.m.
May to November
800.897.FARM

Corte Madera CFM
Town Center Central Courtyard
Tamalpais Dr., at Paradise
Wednesdays, 1 p.m. to 6 p.m.
415.382.7846

Fairfax CFM
Fairfax Theater Parking Lot
Broadway Blvd., at Sir Francis
    Drake Blvd.
Wednesdays, 4 p.m. to 8 p.m.
May through October
800.897.FARM

San Rafael Downtown CFM
4th St. & B
Thursdays, 6 p.m. to 9 p.m.
April through September
415.457.2266

San Rafael Thursday Marin
County CFM, Civic Center
San Pedro Rd., at Hwy. 101
Thursdays, 8 a.m. to 1 p.m.
800.897.FARM

Sausalito CFM
Bridgeway & Tracy
Fridays, 4 p.m. to 8 p.m.
June to September
415.382.7846

Larkspur CFM
Larkspur Landing Circle
Saturdays, 10 a.m. to 2 p.m.
June through November
415.382.7846

Pt. Reyes Station, W. Marin CFM
Toby's Feed Barn—15479 State
    Route 1
Saturdays, 9 a.m. to 1 p.m.
June through November
415.663.1223

San Geronimo Valley CFM
Valley Presbyterian Church
Sir Francis Drake Blvd., at
    Nicascio Valley Rd.
Saturdays, 9:30 a.m. to 1:30 p.m.
May through October
415.488.4746

San Rafael Sunday Marin
County CFM
Civic Center—Hwy. 101 & San Pedro
Sundays, 8 a.m. to 1 p.m.
800.897.FARM

Napa County

Napa Downtown CFM
COPIA P.L. / 500 First St.
Tuesdays, 7:30 a.m. to noon
May through October
707.252.7142

Yountville CFM
"Compadres" Parking Lot
6539 Washington St., at Humbolt
Wednesdays, 4 p.m. to 8 p.m.
June through August
707.944.0834

Napa Chef's CFM
1st & Main
Fridays, 4 p.m. to 8 p.m.
May through August
707.252.7142

St. Helena Napa Valley CFM
Crane Park
Adams St., at Railroad Ave.
Fridays, 7:30 a.m. to noon
May through October
707.486.2662

Calistoga CFM
1546 Lincoln Ave., at Fair Way
Saturdays, 8:30 a.m. to 12:30 p.m.
June through September
707.829.3494

San Francisco County

San Francisco Ferry Plaza
Garden CFM
Ferry Building—The Embarcadero
Market St., at Steuart
Tuesdays, 10 a.m. to 2 p.m.
415.291.3276

San Francisco Heart of the City CFM
Market St. & 7th
Wednesdays, 7 a.m. to 5:30 p.m.
415.558.9455

San Francisco Ferry Plaza
Garden CFM
Ferry Building—The Embarcadero
Market St., at Steuart
Thursdays, 12 p.m. to dusk
415.291.3276

San Francisco Kaiser CFM
2190 O'Farrell
O'Farrell, at Divisadero
Fridays, 11 a.m. to 3 p.m.
August through November
800.949.FARM

San Francisco Alemany CFM
San Francisco & Putnam
Saturdays, 5 a.m. to 4 p.m.
415.647.9423

San Francisco Bayview CFM
Third & Galvez
Saturdays, 10 a.m. to 3 p.m.
415.285.7584

San Francisco Ferry Plaza CFM
Ferry Building—The Embarcadero
Market St., at Steuart
Saturdays, 8 a.m. to 2 p.m.
415.291.3276

San Francisco Fillmore CFM
Fillmore & Eddy
Saturdays, 8:30 a.m. to 1 p.m
July through November
800.949.FARM

San Francisco Ferry Plaza
Garden CFM
Ferry Building—The Embarcadero
Market St., at Steuart
Sundays, 9 a.m. to 3 p.m.
415.291.3276

San Francisco Heart of the City CFM
Market St. between 7th & 8th
Sundays, 7 a.m. to 5 p.m.
415.558.9455

San Mateo County

San Mateo CFM
College of San Mateo Parking Lot
W. Hilldale, at Csm Dr.
Wednesdays, 9 a.m. to 1 p.m.
800.949.FARM

Daly City CFM
Serramonte Ctr—behind
  Montgomery Wards
Southgate Ave., at Hwy. 280
Thursdays, 9 a.m. to 1 p.m.
800.806.FARM

Half Moon Bay CFM
Cetrella's Restaurant
Main St., at Bloom Ln.
Saturdays, 9 a.m. to 1 p.m.
May through November
650.726.4895

Millbrae CFM
200 Block Broadway, at Victoria
Saturdays, 8 a.m. to 1 p.m.
650.697.7324

Redwood City CFM
Winslow & Middlefield
Saturdays, 7 a.m. to noon
April through November
650.592.4103

S. San Francisco CFM
Orange Memorial Park
W. Orange Ave., at Tennis Dr.
Saturdays, 9 a.m. to 1 p.m.
800.806.FARM

San Mateo CFM
College of San Mateo Parking Lot
W. Hilldale, at Csm Dr.
Saturdays, 9 a.m. to 1 p.m.
800.949.FARM

Belmont CFM
El Camino Real & O'Neill Ave.
Sundays, 9 a.m. to 1 p.m.
May through November
800.949.FARM

Burlingame Fresh Market CFM
Howard Ave. & Park
Sundays, 9 a.m. to 1:30 p.m.
May through November
650.344.1735

Menlo Park CFM
Crane & Chestnut
Sundays, 9:30 a.m. to 1:30 p.m.
831.688.8316

Santa Clara County

Milpitas CFM
Milpitas Town Center Mervyn's
  Parking Lot
E. Calaveras Blvd., at Town
  Center Dr.
Wednesdays, 10 a.m. to 2 p.m.
800.949.FARM

San Jose Santana CFM
Santana Row
Stevens Creek Blvd. &
  Winchester Blvd.
Wednesdays, 4 p.m. to 8 p.m.
800.949.FARM

Sunnyvale CFM
Murphy between Washington &
  Evelyn
Wednesdays, 5 p.m. to 8:30 p.m.
Saturdays, 9 a.m. to 1 p.m.
July to September
510.745.7100

Los Altos CFM
State St. & 2nd St.
Thursdays, 4 p.m. to 8 p.m.
May through September
510.745.7100

San Jose Downtown CFM
San Pedro Square
W. Santa Clara St., at S.
Almaden Blvd.
Fridays, 10 a.m. to 2 p.m.
May through December
800.949.FARM

Vallco Park/Cupertino CFM
Vallco Fashion Park Mall
N. Wolfe Rd., at Stevens
Creek Blvd.
Fridays, 9 a.m. to 1 p.m.
January through November
800.949.FARM

Morgan Hill CFM
Downtown Train Station
3rd & Depot
Saturdays, 9 a.m. to 1 p.m.
May through October
800.806.FARM

Palo Alto Downtown CFM
Gilman, at Hamilton Ave.
Saturdays, 8 a.m. to noon
May through December
650.328.2827

San Jose Willow Glen CFM
Minnesota & Lincoln, at
elementary school
Saturdays, 8:30 a.m. to noon
April to December
408.353.4293

Santa Clara CFM
Jackson & Homestead
Saturdays, 9 a.m. to 1 p.m.
May through October
510.745.7100

Saratoga CFM
Saratoga High School
Saratoga Sunnyvale Rd., at
Herriman Ave.
Saturdays, 9 a.m. to 1 p.m.
800.806.FARM

Campbell CFM
2nd St. & Campbell Ave.
Sundays, 9 a.m. to 1 p.m.
510.745.7100

Los Gatos CFM
Montabello Way & Broadway
Sundays, 8 a.m. to 12:30 p.m.
408.353.4293

Milpitas CFM
Milpitas Town Center, Mervyn's
Parking Lot
E. Calaveras Blvd., at Town
Center Dr.
Sundays, 9 a.m. to 1 p.m.
800.949.FARM

Mountain View CFM
Hope & Evelyn—100 Castro St.
Sundays, 9 a.m. to 1 p.m.
800.806.FARM

San Jose Blossom Hill CFM
Princeton Plaza Mall
Koozer & Meridian
Sundays, 10 a.m. to 2 p.m.
800.806.FARM

San Jose Evergreen CFM
Mirassou Vineyards
3000 Aborn Rd., at N. 2nd St.
Sundays, 9 a.m. to 1 p.m.
May through October
510.745.7100

San Jose Japan Town CFM
Jackson St. between 7th & 8th
Sundays, 8:30 a.m. to noon
408.298.4303

San Jose Santana CFM
Santana Row
Stevens Creek & Winchester
Sundays, 9 a.m. to 2 p.m.
800.949.FARM

Solano County

Vallejo CFM
Georgia & Sonoma
Wednesdays, 4 p.m. to 8 p.m.
June through September
800.949.FARM

Benicia CFM
Downtown First St., between B & D
Thursdays, 4 p.m. to 8 p.m.
April through October
707.745.9791

Fairfield CFM
W. Texas St., at Madison St.
Thursdays, 4 p.m. to 8 p.m.
May through October
707.254.1965

Vacaville CFM
Main St. & Dobbins
Saturdays, 8 a.m. to noon
May through November
800.897.FARM

Vallejo CFM
Georgia & Marin
Saturdays, 9 a.m. to 1 p.m.
800.949.FARM

Sonoma County

Healdsburg CFM
The Plaza, at Healdsburg Ave.
Tuesdays, 4 p.m. to 6:30 p.m.
June through October
707.431.2956

Sonoma Tuesday CFM
Sonoma Plaza, at Napa St.
Tuesdays, 5:30 p.m. to 8:30 p.m.
April through October
707.538.7023

Guerneville CFM
16209 First St., at Hwy. 116
Wednesdays, 4 p.m. to 7 p.m.
May through September
707.865.4171

Santa Rosa Original CFM
Vets Building Parking Lot
1351 Maple, at Brookwood
Wednesdays, 8:30 a.m. to noon
707.522.8629

Santa Rosa Downtown CFM
4th & B Street
Wednesdays, 5 p.m. to 8:30 p.m.
May through August
707.524.2123

Cotati CFM
La Plaza Park, at E. Cotati Ave.
Thursdays, 5 p.m. to 8:30 p.m.
June through October
707.795.5508

Windsor CFM
Bell Rd., at Town Green
Thursdays, 5 p.m. to 8 p.m.
June through August
707.433.4595

Sonoma Friday CFM
Depot Museum Parking Lot
1st & Spain St.
Fridays, 9 a.m. to noon
707.538.7023

Duncan Mills CFM
25300 Steelhead Blvd.
Saturdays, 11 a.m. to 3 p.m.
April through November
707.865.4171

Healdsburg CFM
North & Vine
Saturdays, 9 a.m. to noon
May through November
707.431.1956

Occidental CFM
Community Center
3920 Bohemian Hwy.
Saturdays, 9 a.m. to 12:30 p.m.
May through November
707.874.2242

Petaluma CFM
Walnut Park
4th & D
Saturdays, 2 p.m. to 5 p.m.
May through October
707.762.0344

Santa Rosa Oakmont CFM
Bank Parking Lot
White Oak & Oakmont
Saturdays, 9 a.m. to noon
707.538.7023

Santa Rosa Original CFM
Vets Building Parking Lot
1351 Maple, at Brookwood
Saturdays, 8:30 a.m. to noon
707.522.8629

Sebastopol CFM
New Town Plaza, by
   Sebastopol Ave.
Sundays, 10 a.m. to 1:30 p.m.
April through December
707.522.9305

Windsor CFM
Bell Rd., at Town Green
Sundays, 10 a.m. to 1 p.m.
May through November
707.433.4595

GREEN GROCERS

Berkeley

Andronico's
2655 Telegraph Avenue, Berkeley
510.845.1062
Full service high-end grocery

Andronico's
1850 Solano Avenue, Berkeley
510.524.1673

Andronico's
1414 University Avenue, Berkeley
510.548.7061

Andronico's
1550 Shattuck Avenue, Berkeley
510.841.7942

Berkeley Bowl, Berkeley
2020 Oregon Street, Berkeley
510.843.6929
Excellent produce

Monterey Market
1550 Hopkins Street, Berkeley
510.526.6042
Email: info@montereymarket.com
Near-legendary produce market

Musashi Market
2126 Dwight Way, Berkeley
510.843.2017
Japanese ingredients, including seaweeds

Whole Foods Market
3000 Telegraph Avenue, Berkeley
510.649.1333

Boulder Creek

New Leaf Community Market
13159 Hwy 9, Boulder Creek
831.338.7211

Burlingame

Earthbeam Natural Foods
1399 Broadway Street, Burlingame
650.347.2058

Mollie Stone's Market
1477 Chapin Avenue, Burlingame
650.558.9992
Full service high-end grocery

Campbell

Whole Foods Market
1690 S. Bascom Avenue, Campbell
408.371.5000

Capitola

New Leaf Community Market
1210 41st Avenue, Capitola
831.479.7987
Website: www.newleaf.com

Castro Valley

Health Unlimited Health Food
3446 Village Drive, Castro Valley
510.581.0220

Concord

Harvest House
2395 Monument Boulevard, Concord
925.676.2305
Natural food store

Corte Madera

Paradise Foods
5627 Paradise Drive, Corte Madera
415.945.8855

Cotati

Oliver's Market
546 East Cotati Avenue, Cotati
707.795.9501
Full-service grocery; large prepared foods section.

Cupertino

Cupertino Natural Foods
10255 South De Anza Boulevard, Cupertino
408.253.1277

Whole Foods Market
20830 Stevens Creek Boulevard, Cupertino
408.257.7000

Danville

Andronico's
345 Railroad Avenue, Danville
925.855.8920

El Cerrito

El Cerrito Natural Grocery
10367 San Pablo Avenue, El Cerrito
510.526.1155

Emeryville

Andronico's
6529 Hollis Street, Emeryville
510.658.3377

Fairfax

Good Earth Natural Foods
1966 Sir Francis Drake Boulevard, Fairfax
415.454.0123

Felton

New Leaf Community Market
6240 Hwy 9, Felton
831.335.7322

Fremont

Fremont Natural Foods
5180 Mowry Avenue, Fremont
510.792.0163

Glen Ellen

Glen Ellen Village Market
13751 Arnold Drive, Glen Ellen
707.996.6728

Greenbrae

Mollie Stone's Market
270 Bon Air Shopping Center, Greenbrae
415.461.1164

Guerneville

Food for Humans
16385 First Street, Guerneville
707.869.3612

Half Moon Bay

Half Moon Bay Natural Foods
523 Main Street, Half Moon Bay
650.726.7881

Healdsburg

Anstead's Marketplace & Deli
428 Center Street, Healdsbug
707.431.0530

Oakville Grocery
124 Matheson Street, Healdsburg
707.433.3200

Kentfield

Woodlands Market
735 College Avenue, Kentfield
415.457.8160

Kenwood

Kenwood Village Market
8910 Sonoma Hwy, Kenwood
707.833.4801

Los Altos

Andronico's
690 Los Altos Rancho Center, Los Altos
650.948.6648

Los Gatos

Whole Foods Market
15980 Los Gatos Boulevard, Los Gatos
408.358.4434

Menlo Park

Draeger's Supermarket
1010 University Drive, Menlo Park
650.688.0675
High-end grocery, cookware, cookbooks, cafe

Milpitas

Sugandh India Imports
188 South Abel Street, at Calaveras Boulevard in Abel Plaza,
Milpitas
408.956.9509
Indian ingredients

Mill Valley

Whole Foods Market
414 Miller Avenue, Mill Valley
415.381.1200

Monterey

Whole Foods Market
800 Del Monte Center, Monterey
831.333.1600

Napa

Brown's Valley Market
2362 Brown's Valley Road, Napa
707.253.1873

Golden Carrot Natural Foods
River Park Shopping Center
1621 West Imola Avenue, Napa
707.224.3117
General market, juice bar, prepared foods

Nob Hill Foods
611 Trancas, Napa
707.224.8583

Optimum Natural Foods
633 Trancas, Napa
707.224.1514

Oakland

Farmer Joe's Produce & Marketplace
3501 Macarthur Boulevard, Oakland
510.482.8178
Produce, faux meats, Asian ingredients, vegan products

Food Mill
3033 Macarthur Boulevard, Oakland
510.482.3848
Faux meats

Layonna Vegetarian Health Food Market
443 8th Street, at Broadway, Oakland
510.763.3168
Faux meats, vegan ingredients

The Pasta Shop
5655 College Avenue, at Rockridge, Oakland
510.547.4005
High-end market

Piedmont Grocery
4038 Piedmont Avenue, Oakland
510.653.8181

Oakville

Oakville Grocery Napa Valley
7856 St. Helena Highway, Oakville
707.944.8802
Original location; excellent cheeses, olive oils, vinegars,
    organic, produce

Pacifica

Good Health Natural Foods
80 West Manor Drive, Pacifica
650.355.5936

Palo Alto

Andronico's
500 Stanford Shopping Center, Palo Alto
650.327.5505

Oakville Grocery
715 Stanford Shopping Center, Palo Alto
650.328.9000

Whole Foods Market
774 Emerson Street, Palo Alto
650.326.8676

Petaluma

Petaluma Market
210 Western Avenue, Petaluma
707.762.5464

Whole Foods Market
621 E. Washington, Petaluma
707.762.9352

San Anselmo

Andronico's
100 Center Boulevard, San Anselmo
415.455.8186

Piccadilly Circus
222 Greenfield Avenue, San Anselmo
415.258.0660
General market, cafe, juice bar, organic produce

San Bruno

Mollie Stone's Market
22 Bayhill Shopping Center, San Bruno
650.873.8075

San Francisco

Andronico's
1200 Irving Street, San Francisco
415.661.3220

Fresh Organics
3939 24th Street, San Francisco
415.282.9500

Fresh Organics
5843 Geary Boulevard, San Francisco
415.387.6367

Fresh Organics
1001 Stanyan Street, San Francisco
415.564.2800

Mollie Stone's Market
2435 California Street, San Francisco
415.567.3215

Otsu
3253 16th Street, San Francisco
415.255.7900
866.HEY.OTSU (toll-free)
Email: info@veganmart.com
Vegan products, including shoes, hats, wallets, and all
  manner of other goodies to compliment the complete
  vegan lifestyle

Rainbow Grocery Cooperative
1745 Folsom Street, San Francisco
415.663.0620
Website: www.rainbow.coop
Cooperative full-service grocery

Whole Foods Market
399 4th Street, San Francisco
415.618.0066

San Mateo

Draeger's Supermarket
222 East 4th Avenue, San Mateo
650.685.3700
High-end grocery, cookware, cookbooks, cafe

Mollie Stone's
49 West 42nd Avenue, San Mateo
650.372.2839

Whole Foods Market
1010 Park Place, San Mateo
650.358.6900

Santa Cruz

New Leaf Community Market
2351 Mission Avenue, Santa Cruz
831.426.1306

New Leaf Community Market Downtown
1134 Pacific Avenue, Santa Cruz
831.425.1793

Santa Rosa

Oliver's Market
560 Montecito Centre, Santa Rosa
707.537.7123

Pacific Market
1465 Town & Country Drive, Santa Rosa
707.546.3663

Santa Rosa Community Market
1899 Mendocino Avenue, near Elliot Avenue, Santa Rosa
707.546.1806

Whole Foods Market
1181 Yulupa Avenue, Santa Rosa
707.575.7915

Saratoga

Natural Instincts
14435 Big Basin Way, Saratoga
408.867.9670
Natural Food Store

Sausalito

Mollie Stone's Market
100 Harbor Drive, Sausalito
415.331.6900

Sonoma

Sonoma Market
500 W. Napa Street, Suite 550, Sonoma
707.996.3411

Sebastopol

Andy's Produce Market
1691 Hwy 116 North, Sebastopol
707.823.8661

Fiesta Market
550 Gravenstein Hwy, Sebastopol
707.823.9735

Whole Foods Market
6910 McKinley Street, Sebastopol
707.829.9801

St. Helena

Dean & DeLuca
607 St. Helena Hwy, St. Helena
707.967.9980

Sunshine Foods
1115 Main Street, St. Helena
707.963.7070

Walnut Creek

Andronico's
1181 Locust Street, Walnut Creek
925.977.1966

Whole Foods Market
1333 E. Newell, Walnut Creek
925.274.9700

Juice Bars, Cheese Shops, Bakeries

Benicia

The Cheese Shop
1075 1st Street, Benicia
707.746.6818

Berkeley

Acme Bread Company
1607 San Pablo Avenue, Berkeley
510.843.2978

Acme Bread Company
2730 9th Street, Berkeley
510.843.1695

The Cheese Board Collective
1504 Shattuck Avenue at Vine, Berkeley
510.549.3183
Artisan cheeses, baked goods

Healdsburg

The Cheese Shop
423 Center Street, Healdsburg
707.433.4998

Los Gatos

Juice It
81 West Main Street, Los Gatos
408.395.2333

Mill Valley

The Cheese Shop
38 Miller Avenue, Suite 7, Mill Valley
415.383.7272

Oakland

Ital Kalabash Juice Bar & Restaurant
1405 Franklin Street, near 14th, Oakland
510.836.4825

Your Black Muslim Bakery
5832 San Pablo Avenue, Oakland
510.658.7080

Your Black Muslim Bakery
365 17th Street, Oakland
510.839.1313

Your Black Muslim Bakery
Oakland Coliseum Entrance C
Space 109, Oakland
No phone

Your Black Muslim Bakery
Oakland Airport Terminal #2, Oakland
510.639.7490

Point Reyes Station

Cowgirl Creamery at Tomales Bay Foods
80 4th Street, Point Reyes Station
415.663.8153

Rohnert Park

Juice Works
969 Golf Course Drive, Rohnert Park
707.585.8229

San Francisco

Cowgirl Creamery Artisan Cheese
San Francisco Ferry Plaza
1 Ferry Plaza, at the Embarcadero, San Francisco
415.362.9354

Cowgirl Creamery Artisan Cheese
2413 California Street, at Fillmore, San Francisco
415.929.8610

Juicy News
2453 Fillmore at Jackson, San Francisco
415.441.3851

Your Black Muslim Bakery
609 Cole at Haight, San Francisco
415.387.6384

Santa Rosa

Juice Shack
1018 Mendocino Avenue, Santa Rosa
707.528.6131

Juice Shack
2154 Santa Rosa Avenue, Santa Rosa
707.522.6289

PB & J Cafe—Juice 'n' Java
2101 W. College Avenue, Suite H, Santa Rosa
707.568.7472

Squeezer's Juice Bar
519 4th Street, near Mendocino, Santa Rosa
707.573.8080

Team Juice
2700 Yulupa, Santa Rosa
707.546.3550

Sebastopol

Difruitti's Juicery
6988 McKinley, Sebastopol
707.829.3989

Village Bakery
7225 Healdsburg Avenue, Sebastopol
707.829.8101

Sonoma

Artisan Bakers
750 West Napa Avenue, Sonoma
707.939.1765

The Cheese Maker's Daughter
127 E. Napa, Sonoma
707.996.4060

Vella Cheese Company
315 Second Street E., Sonoma
707.938.3232, 800.848.0505
www.vellacheese.com

Walnut Creek

Walnut Creek Baking Company
1686 Locust, Walnut Creek
925.988.9222

COOKING SCHOOLS AND CLASSES

These locations offer cooking classes, many of which feature vegetarian cuisine, to consumers throughout the year. Some also offer professional courses.

Berkeley

Sur La Table
1806 Fourth Street
Berkeley
510.849.2252
www.surlatable.com

Danville

Andronico's
karen.alvarez@andronicos.com

Cooks and Books and Corks
148 E. Prospect Avenue
Danville
925.831.0708

Healdsburg

Relish Culinary School
P.O. Box 933
Healdsburg, CA 95448
707.431.9999
www.relishculinary.com

Los Gatos

Sur La Table
23 University Avenue
Los Gatos
408.395.6946

Menlo Park

Draeger Epicureans
1010 University Drive
Menlo Park
650.324.7751

Sonoma

Ramekins Sonoma Valley
Culinary School
450 W. Spain Street
Sonoma
707.933.0450
www.ramekins.com

San Francisco

Sur La Table
77 Maiden Lane
San Francisco
415.732.7900

Tante Marie's Cooking School
271 Francisco Street
San Francisco, CA 94133
415.788.6699
www.tantemarie.com

San Mateo

Draeger's
222 East 4th Avenue
San Mateo
650.685.3795

Santa Rosa

Santa Rosa Junior College
Culinary Center
7th & B Street
Santa Rosa
707.524.7886
www.santarosa.edu

Sur La Table
Montgomery Center
2323 Mogowan Drive
Santa Rosa
Opening June 2004

Walnut Creek

Andronico's Food & Event
*   Center*
karen.alvarez@andronicos.com

Vegetarian Societies

Some restaurants included in this book offer discounts to members of vegetarian societies. More importantly, these societies offer information and support to the new vegetarian.

Alameda County

East Bay Vegetarians
P.O. Box 5450
Oakland, CA 94605
510.562.9934
www.howarddy2@usa.net

Lesbian Vegetarian Group
510.236.4453

Contra Costa County

Contra Costa Vegetarians
Meets on 3rd Saturdays
510.671.2413

Marin County

EarthSave Marin
P.O. Box 2874
San Anselmo, CA 94979
415.383.9143
www.marin@earthsave.org

Sacramento County

Sacramento Raw
Sacramento, CA 95814
916.442.1498
www.rawsacramento.net

Sacramento Vegetarian Society
P.O. Box 163583
Sacramento, CA 95816
916.554.7090
www.home.earthlink.net/~
sacveggie/

San Francisco County

Bay Area Jewish Vegetarians
www.ivu.org/bajv/

San Francisco Living Foods Enthusiasts
662 29th Avenue
San Francisco, CA 94121
415.751.2806
www.living-foods.com/sflife/index.html

San Francisco Vegetarian Society
P.O. Box 2510
San Francisco, CA 94126
415.273.5481
www.sfvs.org

San Mateo County

EarthSave Bay Area
P.O. Box 70205
Sunnyvale, CA 94086
408.380.1214
www.bayarea.earthsave.org

EarthSave International
1509 Seabright Avenue, Suite B1
Santa Cruz, CA 95062
831.423.0293
800.362.3648
www.earthsave.org

Peninsula Macrobiotic Community
Palo Alto
650.599.3320
www.peninsulamacro.org

Santa Clara County

EarthSave Bay Area
P.O. Box 865
Cupertino, CA 95015
408.380.1214
www.bayarea@earthsave.org

Sonoma County

North Bay Living Foods
    Community
P.O. Box 7443
Cotati, CA 94931
707.793.2365
www.beraw.com

Vegetarians of Sonoma
    County
P.O. Box 4003
Santa Rosa, CA 95402
707.528.2892

Regional

Bay Area Active Asian
    Vegetarians
BayAreaAsianVeg-
subscribe@yahoogroups.com

Bay Area Vegetarians
www.bayareaveg.org

Bay Area Young Vegetarians
www.groups.yahoo.com/group/
bayareayoungvegetarians/
20s to 30s (must join
through Yahoo)

Community Alliance with
    Family Farmers
P.O. Box 363
Davis, CA 95617
707.756.7857
caff@caff.org
www.caff.org
Non-profit organization that
    links individuals, families,
    and farmers

Gay and Lesbian Vegetarians
    of North California (GLVNC)
www.dolphyn.com/qveg/
glvnc.htm

LifeGarden
860 Bellows Ct.
Walnut Creek, CA 94596
925.937.3044
info@lifegarden.org
www.lifegarden.org
Educational nonprofit
    organization that focuses
    on community garden
    projects, including in
    schools

North Bay Vegetarian Society
emarie2112@aol.com

Vegetarian Resource Group
www.vrg.org

ALPHABETICAL INDEX

All You Knead, 68

Amarin Thai Cuisine, 126

Ambrosia Garden, 58

Amira Restaurant, 69

Ananda Fuara, 70

Angkor Borei, 71

Annapurna Restaurant, 146

Ashkenaz Community Center, 16

Bangkok Bay Thai, 116

Bangkok Cuisine, 117

Bistro Don Giovanni, 59

Bok Choy Gardens, 72

Breads of India & Gourmet Curries, 17

Cafe Fanny, 18

Caffe Oggi, 42

Chai Baba Chai, 147

Cha-Ya, 19

Cheese Board Pizza Collective, The, 20

Chez Panisse Cafe, 21

China Wok, 127

Cool Café, The, 118

Crepevine, 22, 73, 74, 119

Cucina Paradiso, 148

Dasaprakash, 128

Dee Dee's Indian Fast Food, 129

Dempsey's Restaurant and Brewery, 149

Dharmas Natural Foods, 130

Downtown Bakery & Creamery, 150

East West Bakery & Cafe, 151, 152

Eat-A-Pizza, 23

Einstein's Cafe, 75

El Camino Bueno Bueno Burritoria, 131

Ephesus Kebab Lounge, 60

Ethiopian Restaurant, 24

Flea Street Cafe, 120

Fleur de Lys, 76

Fork, 43

Garden Fresh Restaurant, 132

Golden Era Vegetarian Restaurant, 77

Golden Lotus Vegetarian Restaurant, 25

Govinda's, 153

Green Gulch Farm, 44

Greens, 78

Haveli, 79

Herbivore, 80, 81

Hulu House, 82

India Village, 45

Jay's Cheesesteak, 83, 84

Jhan Thong, 46

JhanThong Banbua, 154

Jimtown Store, 155

Joy Meadow Restaurant, 121

Juice Bar Collective, 26

Juicy Lucy's, 85

Julia's Kitchen at COPIA, 61

Junkang-Restaurant at City of 10,000 Buddhas, 54

jZCool Eatery & Catering Co., 122

K & L Bistro, 156

Kan Zaman, 86

Kokila Kitchen, 133

Komala Vilas, 134

Krishna Restaurant, 12

La Fondue, 135

Latino's Pupuseria &
    Restaurante El Salvador, 62

Long Life Vegi House, 27

Lotus, 47

Lucky Creation, 87

Lu Lai Garden, 136

Lydia's Lovin' Food, 48

Mandalay Restaurant, 88

Meant to Be Music, 28

Milan Sweet Center, 137

Millennium, 89

Miss Millie's, 90

Mystic Isle Cafe, 157

Nan Yang Rockridge, 29

Nature's Bounty, 55

New Ganges Restaurant, 91

New World Vegetarian, 30

Noodle King, 138

North Light Books and Cafe,
    158

OlivetoDownstairs & Cafe, 31

Organic Cafe & Macrobiotic
    Market, 32

Parkside Cafe, 49

Passage to India, 139

Piperade, 92

Piperade Cafe, 93

Q, 94

Raven Restaurant, The, 56

Raw Energy Organic Juice
    Cafe, 33

Razan's Kitchen, 34

Reggae Runnins Village and
    Restaurant, 95

Roxanne's 50

Roxanne's-To-Go, 51

Samovar Tea Lounge, 96

San Francisco Soup
    Company, The, 97–102

Saravana Bhavan, 140

Seaweed Cafe, 159

Shangri-La, 103

Sher-e-Punjab, 52

Shoreline Bueno Bueno
    Burritoria, 141

Sizzling Tandoor, 160

Slice of Life, 161

Small World, 63

Smart Alec's Intelligent
    Food, 35

Soups, 104

Sparks, 162

Stoa Restaurant & Bar, 123

Sue's Indian, 142

Sunrise Deli, 105

Taste of Africa, A, 36

Thai House, 163

Truly Mediterranean, 106, 107

2002 Oxygen Bar, 108

Udupi Palace, 13, 37, 143

Urban Forage, 109

Vege House, 38, 110

Vegevillage, 64

Vegi Food, 39

Vicolo Pizza, 111

Vietnamese Sandwiches, 112

Vik's Chaat Corner, 40

Water Street Bistro, 164

Wine Spectator Restaurant,
    65

Zante Pizza and Indian
    Cuisine, 113

CUISINE INDEX

African
A Taste of Africa, 36

American
All You Knead, 68

Jay's Cheesesteak, 83, 84

Juice Bar Collective, 26

Miss Millie's, 90

Q, 94

Smart Alec's Intelligent Food, 35

Asian
Joy Meadow Restaurant, 121

Bakery
Downtown Bakery & Creamery, 150

Basque
Piperade, 92

Burmese
Mandalay Restaurant, 88

Nan Yang Rockridge, 29

California-French
Chez Panisse Cafe, 21

Fork, 43

Julia's Kitchen at COPIA, 61

Seaweed Cafe, 159

Water Street Bistro, 164

Californian
Cafe Fanny, 18

Chez Panisse Cafe, 21

The Cool Café, 118

Dempsey's Restaurant and Brewery, 149

Einstein's Cafe, 75

Flea Street Cafe, 120

Fork, 43

Greens, 78

Jimtown Store, 155

Julia's Kitchen at COPIA, 61

jZCool Eatery & Catering Co., 122

Mystic Isle Cafe, 157

Nature's Bounty, 55

North Light Books and Cafe, 158

Parkside Cafe, 49

The Raven's Restaurant, 56

Seaweed Cafe, 159

Stoa Restaurant & Bar, 123

Water Street Bistro, 164

Wine Spectator Restaurant, 65

Cambodian
Angkor Borei, 71

Cantonese
Ambrosia Garden, 58

Chinese
Bok Choy, 72

China Wok, 127

Golden Lotus Vegetarian Restaurant, 25

Long Life Vegi House, 27

Lu Lai Garden, 136

Lucky Creation, 87

Noodle King, 138

Shangri-La, 103

Vege House, 38, 110

Vegi Food, 39

Ethiopian
Ethiopian Restaurant, 24

Fondue
La Fondue, 135

French
Chez Panisse Cafe, 21

Fleur de Lys, 76

Fork, 43

Julia's Kitchen at COPIA, 61

K & L Bistro, 156

Seaweed Cafe, 159

Water Street Bistro, 164

Himalayan
Annapurna Restaurant, 146

Indian
Breads of Life India &
  Gourmet Curries, 17

Dasaprakash, 128

Dee Dee's Indian Fast Food,
  129

Garden Fresh Restaurant, 132

Haveli, 79

India Village, 45

Kokila Kitchen, 133

Komala Vilas, 134

Krishna Restaurant, 12

Lotus, 47

Milan Sweet Center, 137

New Ganges Restaurant, 91

Passage to India, 139

Saravana Bhavan, 140

Sher-e-Punjab, 52

Sizzling Tandoor, 160

Sue's Indian, 142

Udupi Palace, 13, 37, 143

Vik's Chaat Corner, 40

Zante Pizza and Indian
  Cuisine, 113

International
Ananda Fuara, 70

Ashkenaz Community
  Center, 16

Chai Baba Chai, 147

Dharmas Natural Foods, 130

East West Bakery & Cafe,
  151-52

Govinda's, 153

Herbivore, 80, 81

Lydia's Lovin' Food, 48

Meant to Be Music, 28

Millennium, 89

New World Vegetarian, 30

Razan's Kitchen, 34

Samovar Tea Lounge, 96

Slice of Life, 161

Sparks, 162

Italian
Bistro Don Giovanni, 59

Caffe Oggi, 42

Cucina Paradiso, 148

OlivetoDownstairs & Cafe, 31

Jamaican
Reggae Runnins Village
  Store and Restaurant, 95

Japanese
Cha-Ya, 19

Juice Bar
Juice Bar Collective, 26

Juicy Lucy's, 85

Lebanese
Sunrise Deli, 105

Mexican-American
El Camino Bueno Bueno
  Burritoria, 131

Shoreline Bueno Bueno
  Burritoria, 141

Middle Eastern
Amira Restaurant, 69

Crepevine, 22, 73, 74, 119

Eat-A-Pita, 23

Kan Zaman, 86

Small World, 63

Truly Mediterranean, 106-7

Organic
Raw Energy Organic Juice
  Cafe, 33

Razan's Kitchen, 34

Pizzeria
The Cheese Board Pizza
  Collective, 20

Vicolo Pizza, 111

Zante Pizza and Indian
  Cuisine, 113

Raw Vegan
Roxanne's, 50

Roxanne's-To-Go, 51

Urban Forage, 109

Raw Vegetarian
Organic Cafe & Macrobiotic
  Market, 32

2202 Oxygen Bar, 108

Salvadoran
Latino's Pupuseria &
  Restaurante El Salvador, 62

Singaporean
Hulu House, 82

Soup
The San Francisco Soup
  Company, 97-102

Soups, 104

Taiwanese
Ambrosia Garden, 58

Vegevillage, 64

Thai
Amarin Thai Cuisine, 126

Bangkok Bay Thai, 116

Bangkok Cuisine, 117

Jhan Thong, 46

JhanThong Banbua, 154

Thai House, 163

Turkish
Ephesus Kebab Lounge, 60

Vietnamese
Golden Era Vegetarian
  Restaurant, 77

Golden Lotus Vegetarian
  Restaurant, 25

Noodle King, 138

Vege House, 38, 110

Vietnamese Sandwiches, 112

Top 10 Index

Top 10 for Food

1. Chez Panisse Café, 21
2. Roxanne's/Roxanne's-To-Go, 50–51
3. Millennium, 89
4. Fleur de Lys, 76
5. Fork, 43
6. Stoa Restaurant & Bar, 123
7. The Ravens Restaurant, 56
8. Cha-Ya, 19
9. Nan Yang Rockridge, 29
10. Junkang-Restaurant, 54

Top 10 for Atmosphere

1. Jimtown Store, 155
2. Einstein's Café, 75
3. Greens, 78
4. Miss Millie's, 90
5. 2202 Oxygen Bar, 108
6. Fleur de Lys, 76
7. Samovar Tea Lounge, 96
8. Green Gulch Farm, 44
9. La Fondue, 135
10. Seaweed Cafe, 159

Top 10 Best Buys

1. Cheese Board Pizza Collective, The, 20
2. Juice Bar Collective, 26
3. jZCool Eatery, 122
4. Organic Cafe & Macrobiotic Market, 32
5. Juicy Lucy's, 85
6. Ananda Fuara, 70
7. Urban Forage, 109
8. Hulu House, 82
9. Piperade Cafe, 93
10. Bok Choy Gardens, 72